OF LIFE IMMENSE

•THE PROPHETIC VISION OF WALT WHITMAN•

RONALD KNAPP

*To Regen
A chance to you
to know Walt Whitman
From
Ron Knapp*

Outskirts Press, Inc.
Denver, Colorado

The opinions expressed in this manuscript are solely the opinions of the author and do not represent the opinions or thoughts of the publisher. The author represents and warrants that s/he either owns or has the legal right to publish all material in this book.

Of Immense Life
The Prophetic Vision of Walt Whitman

All Rights Reserved.
Copyright © 2008 Ronald Knapp
V3.0

This book may not be reproduced, transmitted, or stored in whole or in part by any means, including graphic, electronic, or mechanical without the express written consent of the publisher except in the case of brief quotations embodied in critical articles and reviews.

Outskirts Press, Inc.
http://www.outskirtspress.com

ISBN: 978-1-4327-1260-0

Outskirts Press and the "OP" logo are trademarks belonging to Outskirts Press, Inc.

PRINTED IN THE UNITED STATES OF AMERICA

TABLE OF CONTENTS

Prologue: The Poet As Prophet   1

Chapter I: One's Self I Sing   15

Chapter II: A Place In The Procession   23

Chapter III: The Form Complete   33

Chapter IV: All Were Lacking, If Sex Were Lacking   45

Chapter V: Carols For Comrades And Lovers   61

Chapter VI: For Life, Mere Life   77

Chapter VII: Nothing Else But Miracles   91

Chapter VIII: The Centre Of All Days   103

Chapter IX: Where The Great City Stands   117

Chapter X: Journeyers With Their womanhood   135

Chapter XI: No More The Sad Unnatural Sounds Of War   153

Chapter XII: Science, To You The first Honors Always   169

Chapter XIII: The Truths Of The Earth Continually Wait   181

Chapter XIV: Nature and Humanity Disjoin'd No More   193

Chapter XV: A Vast Similitude Interlocks All   205

Chapter XVI: Death Is The Harvest   219

Chapter XVII: The Road Is Before Us   235

Epilogue: The Germs of A Greater Religion   251

Bibliography and Acknowledgements   253

PROLOGUE
WALT WHITMAN: THE POET AS PROPHET

> The immortal poets of Asia and Europe have done
> their work and pass'd to other spheres,
> A work remains, a work of surpassing all that
> they have done.
> "By Blue Ontario's Shore"

A

"The great construction of the new Bible," Walt Whitman wrote in his journal in the summer of 1857, just two years after the publication of the first edition of <u>Leaves of Grass</u>, "not to be diverted from the principal object – the main life – the three hundred and sixty five...." From the very beginning, from the time he began writing the poems found in <u>Leaves of Grass</u>, Whitman saw himself as undertaking the audacious task of writing a new Bible for the modern world. The reference to the "three hundred and sixty-five" is, obviously, reference to some plan to write three hundred and sixty-five poems for the new Bible – a poem, that is, for each day in the year.

Three decades later, as he approached the end of his life, he added, in "A Backward Glance o'er Travel'd Roads,"

> No one will get at my verses who insists upon viewing them as a literary performance, or attempt at such a performance, or aiming mainly toward art or aestheticism.

It is clear from this passage, and from many others found in his works, that Walt Whitman wanted to be judged, not in terms of the art of his poetry, but in terms of the authenticity of his new Bible, in terms of the validity of his religious vision. The supreme task of the modern poet, Whitman felt, is to be a prophet.

To understand Walt Whitman, as either a man or a poet, one must understand what Whitman himself took to be his own primary purpose. "I re-examine philosophies and religions," he says in "Song of the Open Road," "They may prove well in lecture-rooms, yet not prove at all under the spacious clouds and along the landscape and flowing currents." Walt Whitman desired to create a new "landscape" for a new religion in a new world.

Walt Whitman was not a "religious" person in the ordinary use of that word. He was never much involved in churches or other formal religious institutions. He was in fact often very critical of organized religion. "A lot of churches, sects, etc.," the poet says in <u>Democratic Vistas</u>, are "the most dismal phantasms I know, usurp the name of religion." Whitman saw the development of religion in the modern world as being in an "arrested state," as being locked into outmoded ideas and forms. "There will soon be no more priests," Whitman wrote in the preface to the first edition of <u>Leaves of Grass</u>,

> Their work is done. A new order shall arise and they shall be the priests of man, and every man shall be his own priest. The churches built under their umbrage shall be the churches of men and women. Through the divinity of themselves shall the kosmos and the new breed of poets be interpreters of men and women and of all events and things.

Religion was in need of reform and Whitman saw his own calling as being a religious reformer. The poet defined his own calling in religious terms as in "Starting From Paumanok" where he wrote: "I too, followed by many, and followed many, inaugurate a religion." Although he was connected with no organized religious movement, Whiteman may well be the most deeply religious person in the history of American literature.

B

Walt Whitman saw himself as a prophet in the tradition of the great prophets of the numerous religious traditions of the world, and especially of the great Hebrew prophets. Whitman's view of prophecy is expressed in a commentary on Carlyle, which seems to indicate, as well, a perception of his own purpose. "The word prophecy is much misused; it seems narrow'd to prediction merely," he wrote,

> That is not the main sense of the Hebrew word translated Prophet; it means one whose mind bubbles up and pours forth as a fountain, from inner divine spontaneities revealing God. Prediction is a very minor part of prophecy. The great matter is to reveal and outpour the Godlike suggestions pressing for birth in the soul.

One cannot read Leaves of Grass without being struck by the thought that Whitman's own mind "bubbles up and pours forth as a fountain," and that he is seeking to express "God-like suggestions pressing for birth in [his] soul."

Whitman inherited this view of the prophet, and of prophecy, as he notes, from the Quaker religion of his mother's family, and especially from the preaching of Elias

Hicks, a prominent liberal Quaker heretic of the first half of the nineteenth century. As a boy, Whitman went with his parents to hear Hicks preach and the person and the ideas of this great preacher remained with the poet all of his life.

In a vignette on Hicks, written late in Whitman's life, the poet commented on the ideas of the famed heretic. Hicks "believ'd little in a church as organiz'd---even his own---with houses, ministers, or with salaries, creeds, Sundays, saints, Bibles, holy festivals, etc.," Whitman wrote, "But he believed always in the universal church, in the soul of man, invisibly rapt, ever-waiting, ever-responding to universal truth." This comment on Hicks has seemed to many, and seems to me, to be a comment on himself as well. Whitman felt that he was called to respond to universal truth. Whitman felt the prophetic potential in his own being.

C

Walt Whitman sees himself as a poet/prophet and not as the poet/prophet. That is an important distinction to make. One does Whitman a serious injustice if one sees his vision of the poet/prophet as merely self-serving. Whitman is attempting to call forth a "new breed of poets," as he puts it, who will be "interpreters of men and women and of all events and things," who will accept the challenge to take on the world and articulate a vision of what could be, based on an honest evaluation of what is. There can be many such poets. Indeed, Whitman saw the capacity for the poet/prophet as being latent in every human being. His is a democratic idea. "The messages of great poets to each man and woman are," he says in his preface to the first edition of <u>Leaves of Grass,</u>

Come to us on equal terms, Only then can you understand us, We are no better than you, What we enclose you enclose, What we enjoy you may enjoy. Did you suppose there could be only one Supreme? We affirm there can be unnumbered Supremes, and that one does not countervail another any more than one eyesight countervails another...

Whitman has many synonyms for the poet who accepts his challenge and becomes one of the "Supremes," one of the poet/prophets-- "the greatest poet," "the true poet," "the poet of the Kosmos," "the mature poet," or, in his most poetical, and most audacious form, "the true son of God" – but in each case he is referring to those who accept the challenge to struggle with the world in order to find a meaning that squares with contemporary understanding.

D

Walt Whitman articulates his call for a new breed of poet/prophets, and defines their task, in his preface to the first edition of <u>Leaves of Grass</u>. The poet/prophet is to begin by re-examining "all you have been told at school or church or in any book;" and adds that the poet/prophet should "Dismiss whatever insults your own soul." The true revelation is found in nature, he insists, not in the Bible or any other sacred writing. "Who are you that wanted only to be told what you knew before?" Whitman asks in "By Blue Ontario's Shores," "Who are you that wanted only a book to join you in your nonsense?" The poet/prophet is to begin by ruthlessly re-examining the world and by challenging its fundamental premises. "The poets of the Kosmos," he writes, "advance through all interpositions and coverings and turmoils and stratagems to first principles."

The poet/prophet is to deal with "real things, and real things only;" to love the world we know and can see and can touch and can feel. "The known world has but one complete lover," Whitman says, "and that is the greatest poet." The poet/prophet loves the natural world and pays no attention to the supernatural world. "The whole theory of the special and supernatural and all that was twined with or educed out of it," Whitman says in the preface to the first edition of Leaves of Grass, "departs as a dream." "American needs, and the world needs," Whitman adds in Democratic Vistas,

> a class of bards who will, now and ever, so link and tally the rational physical being of man, with the ensembles of time and space, and with the vast and multiform show, Nature...

The poet/prophet's task is to be honest with what is, and what has been, and to articulate out of that context, what could be. "Past and present and future are no more disjoined but joined," he writes,

> The greatest poet forms the consistence of what is to be from what has been and is. He drags the dead out of their coffins and stands them again on their feet...he says to the past, Rise and walk before me that I may realize you. He learns the lesson...he places himself where the future becomes present.

That phrase – the place "where the future becomes present" – is a singularly powerful phrase. The poet/prophet, although he does not deal with "predictions," deals with what could be in terms of what is. He brings the future into the present and gives it form and beauty and vitality. "Whatever may have been the case in years gone by,"

Whitman says in "A Backward Glance O'er Travel'd Roads," his preface to November Boughs,

> The true use of the imaginative faculty of modern times is to give ultimate vivification to facts, to science...endowing them with glows and glories and final illustriousness which belongs to every real thing, and to real things only.

The poet/prophet has both affection and respect for science, which can be defined in its most fundamental sense as knowledge. The poet/prophet loves knowledge of the world. "Exact knowledge and its practical movements are no check on the greatest poet but always his encouragement and support," Whitman writes, and adds, "There shall be love between the poet and the man of demonstrable science. In the beauty of poems are the tuft and final applause of science." The poet/prophet does not end with science, but that is where one begins. If the poet/prophet is to generate a vision for the future, he needs to do so by beginning with an appreciation for all we have learned up to the present. Great poetry "must in no respect ignore science or modern," Whitman adds in Democratic Vistas,

> but inspire itself with science and the modern. It must bend its vision toward the future, more than the past.

E

The poet/prophet is also "called" to pronounce judgment. "He is no arguer," Whitman says, "He *is* judgment." If the poet/prophet "does not expose superior models and prove himself by every step he takes," Whitman adds, "he is not what is wanted." The poet/prophet examines the world, explores its potential, and makes pronouncements about its meaning – and makes his pronouncements with authority.

Whitman's view of judgment, it seems to me, is one gained from the great tradition of the Hebrew prophets: "Thus saith the Lord." "I hate, I despise your feasts," thunders the great prophet, Amos, "but let justice roll down like waters and righteousness like a mighty stream." It is that stance the poet/prophet is to take. His role is not to argue. His role is to pronounce the Truth! Whitman celebrates this aspect of the poet/prophet in "Song of the Answerer:"

> The words of true poems do not merely please,
> The maker of poems settles justice, reality, immortality;
> His insight and power encircle things and the human race,
> He is the glory and extract thus far of things and of the human race.
> ...
> All this time and at all times wait the words of true poems.
> The words of true poems do not merely please,
> The true poets are not followers of beauty but the august masters of beauty;
> The greatness of sons is the exuding of the greatness of mothers and fathers,
> The words of true poems are the tuft and final applause of science.
> ...
> The words of true poems give you more than poems,
> They give you to form for yourself poems, religions, politics, war, peace, behavior, histories, essays, daily life, and everything else,

They balance ranks, colors, creeds, and the sexes,
They do not seek beauty, they are sought,
  ...
They bring none to his or her terminus or to be content and full,
Whom they take they take into space to behold the birth of stars, to learn one of the meanings,
To launch off with absolute faith, to sweep through the ceaseless rings and never be quiet again.

F

Ralph Waldo Emerson read the first edition of Leaves of Grass shortly after it was published and sent the poet a warm letter of appreciation. "I am not blind to the worth of the wonderful gift of 'Leaves of Grass,' Emerson began, "I find it the most extraordinary piece of wit & wisdom America has yet produced." "I rubbed my eyes a little to see if this sunbeam were no illusion," he continued, "but the solid sense of the book is a sober certainty. It has the best merits, namely, of fortifying & encouraging." "I greet you at the beginning of a great career," he concluded, "which yet must have had a long foreground somewhere for such a start." Emerson's comment about "the long foreground," has long raised the question about Whitman's credentials for his audacious attempt to write a new Bible. What preparations did he undergo to become a poet/prophet? From what sources does he derive his sense of authority?

One does not have to invoke the presence of the supernatural to answer such questions, as did some of his more devout followers a century and more ago. He is not a messiah and he is certainly not a saint. The answer is not found in esoteric theories of "cosmic consciousness" or in ideas of special revelation. The answer is found, rather, in the unique characteristics of his personality, in the experiences of his life, in the nature of his commitment, and in his natural gifts as a poet.

All of his life Walt Whitman had an insatiable curiosity, a well-developed talent for observation, and the unique capacity of absorbing all that he perceived or experienced or read. He was curious about anything and everything and stored it all away for later use in his poetry. Many of his contemporaries, including people in his own family, and later commentators as well, have noted his indolence, his laziness. For many this was seen as a serious flaw, but if it was a flaw, it was one that helped to make a great poet. Whitman spent a great deal of time "loafing" or "sauntering," to use a couple of his own words, but that time provided opportunities to flood the mind with perceptions, images, and information.

In the second stanza of "Song of Myself," the first of his poems, we find these words: "I loafe and invite my soul, I lean and loafe at my ease...observing a spear of summer grass." The image generated by this stanza, if taken to heart, illustrates a fundamental aspect of Whitman's preparation as a poet. Even a blade of grass is to be observed; even a blade of grass has many lessons to teach.

Whitman celebrates his native curiosity and capacity for absorbing all things in a poem called "There Was a Child Went Forth." "There was a child went forth every day, And the first object he look'd upon, that object he became" he began, "And that object became part of him for the day or a certain part of the day, or for many years or stretching cycles of years." After these opening lines Whitman goes into one of his famous, or infamous, catalogues: lists of things the child experienced—"the early lilacs," "the barnyard," "the school mistress," "his own parents," "men and women crowding fast in the streets," "the streets themselves," "the hurrying tumbling waves," "the horizon's edge," dozens of things --- and then concludes, "These became part of that child who went forth every day, and who now goes, and will always go forth every day." The child is clearly Walt Whitman. His preparation for the calling of poet/prophet begins in his childhood, and curiosity, observation, absorption continued throughout his lifetime.

G

Walt Whitman had little formal education but was, nevertheless, a highly educated human being. He had only a few years of grammar school education before he went to work, at the age of eleven, as a clerk in a law office. He was fortunate, in that first job, when one of the younger lawyers took a special interest in him and purchased for him a subscription to a revolving library. From that point on Walt Whitman became a great lover of books and a great lover of knowledge. Throughout his lifetime he read just about everything he could get his hands on. He had a special love of novels, but he was well read in all aspects of English literature --- drama, poetry, literary criticism, essays – and made excursions into other national and cultural literatures as well. He absorbed the Judeo-Christian Bible, and had a great love for it, but he also read widely, as well, in the sacred literature of eastern religions. He immersed himself in history and in biography. He read widely in most of the major branches of science – astronomy, biology, geology, physics, botany, anatomy – and came to possess clear insight into their fundamental premises and theories.

And then there was the city. Walt Whitman was fortunate to spend most of his lifetime in or near the greatest city in the new world, New York. From the time he was a very young "go-fer" for Brooklyn and New York newspapers, he had opportunities to go to the opera, and the theater, and the musical presentations that were part of the night life of that great city. He loved to rummage around in the libraries and the museums and to talk with scholars and curators. People from all of the four corners of the earth frequently found their way to that metropolis---people who were very different from eighteenth century Americans—and Whitman was there to observe and learn.

The poet especially loved the people of the city. He loved to ride the great omnibuses that went up and down Broadway and became friends with the omnibus drivers. Whitman also loved the ferry that connected Brooklyn with New York, making friends with captains and crews and observing people as they went to and fro. He made friends with people from all walks of life: from businessmen to laborers; from the cultural elite to the alien and often illiterate emigrants; from upper-class ladies to prostitutes; from people living in fancy houses to people living in slums. All of these became part of him and became part of the process of defining his prophetic vision.

H

Walt Whitman's prophetic vision was born out of a lifetime of reading, studying, observing, participating, and thinking. It was a lifetime in which he attempted to frame what he had learned in terms of an overarching vision which could give meaning to the modern world.

That vision begins with an exalted view of the self which is seen as sacred, a self in which the body and the soul are one. The vision expands through intimate human relationships and communal relationships and continues, as through a series of concentric circles, until it contains life, the earth, and, ultimately, the universe. Along the way he celebrates human sexuality, incorporates into his vision an ideal democracy with the equality of all persons, and embraces science which has come to define the modern world. Along the way he endeavored to construct a religious understanding which will unite humanity with nature once again and which would see all things—including life and death—as part of a single unfolding universe.

The pages that follow represent an attempt to describe, in systematic form, some of the major themes of the prophetic vision of Walt Whitman. Those themes are presented not from a literary perspective but, as the great poet himself would have wished, from a religious perspective. They are presented with the hope that the reader may gain a greater understanding of Whitman's religious vision of the human universe. They are also presented with the hope that moderns, as we go through the twenty first century, might find in them insights which provide meaning in our own time. Perhaps, like Walt Whitman, we too can come to appreciate a vision of life which is "immense in passion, pulse and power."

CHAPTER I
ONE'S SELF I SING

I celebrate myself and sing myself;
And what I assume you shall assume;
For every atom belonging to me,
 as good belongs to you.
 "Song of Myself"

A

In 1855 a new volume of poetry appeared in some of the bookstores of New York City. It was a curious little book with its bright green cover and its delicate decorations of flowers and plants. The name of the book, as printed on the cover, <u>Leaves of Grass</u>, had roots growing down from the words as if to anchor the book in the earth and branches growing up from the words as if attempting to reach the sky. Inside, following a rambling preface about the poet as prophet, were ten untitled poems. The poems, as they appeared on the page, were different from any other kind of poetry published at that time, with no rhyming pattern, or discernible meter, and with lines that seemed to ramble across the page. The book baffled those who knew poetry. It did not look like poetry, and did not follow the usual protocols of poetry, but it wasn't prose either.

Another curious thing about the book was that it did not

have the author's name on the title page. The first mention of the author appears well into "Song of Myself" where the poet announces himself as

> Walt Whitman, a kosmos, of Manhattan the son,
> Turbulent, fleshy, sensual, eating, drinking and breeding,
> No sentimentalist, no stander above men and women or apart from them,
> No more modest than immodest.

In place of a name on that title page was an engraved picture of a brash young man, dressed in working clothes, with his undershirt showing above his collar, and with his hat cocked to one side. It is the poet as he sees himself – nonchalant, earthy, cocky. It is a visual expression of the lines in the poem by which he introduces himself.

The poet had no publisher. He set the type for the book himself, and had it printed by his friends, the Rome Brothers, in Brooklyn. Not very many copies were sold, and most people who did look at it, decided it was the work of a madman and had no place in the world of poetry. It is said that Emily Dickinson refused to even look at the book, and that Whittier threw his copy into the fireplace. Thus did Walt Whitman introduce himself, and his <u>Leaves of Grass</u>, to the world. Whitman was to spend a lifetime on that book: revising, altering, and adding many poems, as the years went by –nine separate editions in all – and that book, with its strange and humble beginnings was eventually to be recognized as the most important single work of literature in all of American history.

There were ten untitled poems in that first edition of <u>Leaves of Grass</u>, and the first poem, a little later to be called "Walt

Whitman, A Kosmos," and finally, "Song of Myself," took up almost half of the pages. This poem, which is considered by many to be his preeminent masterpiece, provides an entrance into the prophetic vision of Walt Whitman. In all of the numerous editions of <u>Leaves of Grass</u>, "Song of Myself" begins with these words:

> I celebrate myself and sing myself;
> And what I assume you shall assume;
> For every atom belonging to me,
>   as good belongs to you.

In these words are found the foundation stones of Walt Whitman's prophetic vision. To get into that vision we need to understand, line by line, what Whitman intends to say.

B

"I celebrate myself, and sing myself." In "Song of Myself" Walt Whitman is celebrating Walt Whitman. We are in danger of missing Whitman's fundamental point if we pass over, or ignore, this important idea. When the poet says, "I know I am August," he is saying, in a most direct way, "I know that I, Walt Whitman, am august." The dictionary defines "august" as "inspiring awe or admiration; majestic, grand." Walt Whitman is saying that he <u>is</u> "admirable," "majestic," "grand." When Whitman says, "Divine am I, inside and out," he means to point to his own divinity. Even when he writes, humorously I expect, "I dote on myself, there is that lot of me and all so luscious," beneath the humor he is trying to make the point that at the most fundamental level, "Song of Myself" is a celebration of one man, Walt Whitman.

Walt Whitman's prophetic vision begins with Walt

Whitman. <u>Leaves of Grass</u>, Whitman always insisted,

> has been mainly the outcropping of my own emotional nature—an attempt from first to last, to put a person, a human being (myself, in the latter half of the nineteenth century in America) freely, fully and truly on record.

"I should not talk so much about myself," Henry David Thoreau is said to have remarked when challenged about his use of "I" in <u>Walden</u>, "If there were anybody else whom I know as well." Whitman echoed the same kind of thought in "Song of Myself" when he wrote, "One world is aware and by far the largest to me, and that is my self." One has the feeling, however, that unlike Thoreau, Whitman would not have used another word, or another image, even if another word or another image were available to him. Whitman starts with himself because he has no other place to start. Both in terms of his prophetic vision and of his theory of poetics, Whitman discovered that he must begin with the most concrete thing he knows, and that is himself: himself, not as an abstraction, but as a fundamental reality. To understand <u>Leaves of Grass</u>, you have to accept Walt Whitman, "warts and all."

> Apart from the pulling and hauling stands what I am,
> Stands amused, complacent, compassionating, idle, unitary.

Walt Whitman saw himself as "an elemental law" and, as he said, "elemental laws never apologize." There is nothing more "elemental," more solid and concrete – "My foothold is tenon'd and mortis'd in granite" – than oneself; and that self for Whitman is Walt Whitman. He will not apologize for who he is. "At bottom every man knows well enough that he is a unique being," wrote Frederich Niezche,

> only once on this earth; and by no extraordinary chance will such a marvelously picturesque piece of diversity in unity as he is, ever be put together a second time.

Walt Whitman knew that "such a marvelously picturesque piece of diversity" as himself would never be "put together a second time." And he accepted that uniqueness. And insisted that the reader accept it:

> My final merit I refuse you,
> I refuse putting from me what I really am,
> Encompass worlds, but never try to encompass me.

That seems to be the purpose of the photograph, and not a name, on the title page of that first edition of <u>Leaves of Grass</u>. Photography was relatively new in 1855 and for Whitman it provided a more accurate introduction to the poet than his name could provide. A name is an abstraction, and Whitman wanted to avoid abstractions. A picture says more than a thousand words, or so the familiar Chinese adage goes, and I expect that Whitman saw, in that brash photograph, and wanted the reader to see, the real Walt Whitman, or at least what the poet thought was the real Walt Whitman. The poet who was sharing his poems with the world was more than a name; he was a real flesh and blood human being, who recognized his own greatness, who accepted his own uniqueness, and who marveled at his own existence:

> I exist as I am, that is enough,
> I resist any thing better than my own diversity,

> Breathe the air but leave plenty after me,
> And am not stuck up, and in my place.

C

"I celebrate myself, and sing myself," sang Walt Whitman, "And what I assume you shall assume." Everything Walt Whitman says of himself, in terms of his own uniqueness, every other person has the right to "assume," in terms of their own uniqueness. If Whitman thinks that he is majestic and grand, and he does, then every other "self" has the right to assume that they, too, are majestic and grand. Walt Whitman sees himself as the proto-typical human being. He defines himself as a potential model for every other human being. "I am for those who walk abreast of the whole world," Whitman writes in his program poem, "By Blue Ontario's Shore," "who inaugurate one to inaugurate all." The one is himself, but the one stands for all other selves.

"The only self anyone knows is his own," writes the Whitman scholar, Gay Wilson Allen, "But Whitman used himself as a bridge to selfhood." Allen's insightful expression, "a bridge to selfhood," comes closer than any other example I know of in defining Whitman's purpose in the "Song of Myself" motif of <u>Leaves of Grass</u>. Whitman is attempting to provide a bridge from himself to "everyself."

This idea becomes clear, perhaps, when one considers one of the poetic devices Whitman uses to great, and powerful, effect, in many of his poems. When Walt Whitman says "I" he means "I"; he means Walt Whitman. But the reader, in his or her reading, is required to read "I," that is, to appropriate the "I" to himself, or herself. When Whitman says, "I am august," for example, he does mean that Walt Whitman is august. But the reader must also say "I"—I [the reader]—am august. Remember that, for Walt Whitman, the true poems are not in words but in things and in experiences. The true Walt Whitman poem is not in Whitman's words but in the reader's experience of what those words mean. That is why Whitman continually says, "The words of my poems nothing, the drift of them, everything."

In anticipating the charge of egotism, which he expected, and which was hurled at him, Whitman wrote,

> I know perfectly well my own egotism,
> Know my omnivorous lines and must not write any less,
> And would fetch you whoever you are flush with myself.

Walt Whitman would "fetch" the reader "flush" with himself. His egotism is not a solipsistic egotism, but it is a universal one. When Whitman says, "I am larger, better, than I thought," he means that people, individual people, are --- no matter how many millions and millions of such people there are in the world, or have been --- "larger, better" than they sometimes think. Every "self" should recognize its own uniqueness, its own wonder, its own dignity, its own divinity.

D

"Underneath all, individuals," Walt Whitman says in "By Blue Ontario's Shore,"

> I swear nothing is good to me now that ignores individuals,
> The whole theory of the universe is directed

unerringly to one single individual – namely you.

"Underneath the lessons of things, spirits, Nature, governments, ownerships" – anyone who knows Whitman and his lists, knows that he goes on to name a lot of other things, "religions" and "philosophies", for example –

> I swear I perceive other lessons,
> Underneath all to me is myself, to you yourself,
>   (the same monotonous old song.)

This is the ground of Whitman's prophetic vision. The "same monotonous old song," the song of the self, lies at the very heart of his creed. Emerson said that "nothing is at last sacred but the integrity of your own mind." Whitman would say that nothing is at last sacred but the human individual, the human individual as it finds expression in concrete, actual persons, like Walt Whitman and like you and me.

Whitman was primarily interested in individuals and not in that collective abstraction called "humanity." Nothing is more precious, to him, than the individual human being. Emily Dickinson, hearing that it was an obscene work, refused to even look at <u>Leaves of Grass</u>, but she eloquently articulates Whitman's starting place,

> The heart is the capital of the mind –
> The mind is a single state
> The heart and the mind together make
> A single continent –
> One – is the population –
> Numerous enough –
> This ecstatic nation Seek –
> It is yourself.

CHAPTER II
A PLACE IN THE PROCESSION

> I speak the pass-word primeval,
> I give the sign of democracy,
> By God! I will accept nothing which all cannot have
>   their counterpart of on the same terms.
> "Song of Myself"

A

In 1881 Walt Whitman published, in Boston, his sixth edition of <u>Leaves of Grass</u>. This edition, which was published by Charles Osgood, was selling well by the early months of 1882, with 2000 copies in print, and Whitman, for the first time in his life, had some hopes that he might become financially secure. By March of 1882, however, the problems that had constantly recurred throughout his lifetime surfaced once again. On March 4, 1882, Osgood, the publisher, wrote Whitman that the Boston Society For The Suppression of Vice had declared the book to be pornographic and that the book had been withdrawn on order of the state attorney general.

The Massachusetts Attorney General wanted a number of lines revised in the copy of <u>Leaves of Grass</u>, and two poems deleted in their entirety: "A Woman Waits for Me" and "To a Common Prostitute." We shall deal with the first of those two poems, "A Woman Waits for Me," in a later chapter, but "To a Common Prostitute," bears directly on the purpose of this chapter. It is hard to find anything in the poem that could, even remotely, be construed as pornographic, so it seems to have been banned only because it mentioned the forbidden word, "prostitute," and because it did not condemn prostitution.

The attorney general apparently had not read "To a Common Prostitute," or at least had not read it very carefully, because, if he had, he would have noticed that it was a poetic variation on the New Testament story of the woman taken in adultery. In that story, as the reader may remember, the woman is about to be stoned for her sins by a group of men when Jesus intervened. "Let he who is without sin cast the first stone," Jesus said, and one by one the men dropped their stones and walked away. Only Jesus and the woman were left. "Neither do I condemn you," Jesus said, "go and sin no more." Whitman's version is found in "Autumn Rivulets":

> Be composed – be at ease with me –
> I am Walt Whitman, liberal and lusty as nature,
> Not till the sun excludes you do I exclude you,
> Not till the waters refuse to glisten for you and the leaves to rustle for you, do my words refuse to glisten and rustle for you.
>
> My girl I appoint you with an appointment, and I charge you that you make preparation to be worthy to meet me,
> And I charge you that you be patient and perfect till I come.
> Till then I salute you with a significant look that you do not forget me.

Walt Whitman refused to delete this poem, and "A Woman Waits for Me," from his Leaves of Grass and, as had so often happened in the past, the distribution of the book was discontinued. Perhaps the two poems are not, from the perspective of poetry, very good poems, but Whitman always insisted that you could not understand his work if you examined it from the perspective of literature. The idea expressed in these poems, and especially in "To A Common Prostitute," is an idea essential to his prophetic vision. The egalitarian view of the human self, which Whitman proclaims – "Not until the sun excludes you do I exclude you" –insists that even the prostitute, or better, perhaps, the woman that is the prostitute, must be recognized as an authentic human being. "O you shunn'd persons, I at least do not shun you," Whitman says in "Children of Adam,"

> I come forthwith in your midst, I will be your poet,
> I will be more to you than any of the rest.

Whitman had to preserve "To A Common Prostitute," it seems to me, because to delete it would be to water down the central point of his prophetic vision, the sacredness of all human individuals however much they may be "shunn'd," or debased by human society.

B

At the very core of Walt Whitman's prophetic vision, as I have already suggested, is an exalted view of the human individual. In the end "Song of Myself" is not about Walt Whitman – the poet is not the "end" but the "means." "Song of Myself" is a song for everyone to sing. "None has done justice to you," he says in "Birds of Passage," "You have not done justice to yourself." You concern yourself with my arrogance, and with my egotism, he seems to me to be saying, only because you do not realize, as I realize, the wonderful wonderfulness of yourself. It may be you do not understand the elemental truth that,

> Whoever you are, you are he or she for whom the
>   earth is made solid and liquid;
> You are he or she for whom the sun and the stars
>   hang in the sky.

You need to know that you are a central, important, living element in that abstraction called humanity. You are the central, important, living element in that abstraction called democracy. Do justice to yourself! Accept yourself! Sing yourself. Accept the intrinsic value, the august nature of your own being.

"Not till the sun excludes you do I exclude you," Walt Whitman says to the prostitute, in one of the most powerful lines found in all of Leaves of Grass. If the human self is sacred, then the "self" of the prostitute is sacred. And not only the prostitute but every other person who has been denigrated by society. One can go through Leaves of Grass and come up with a whole litany of such people: "the felons on trial in courts," "The convicts in prison cells," "the meanest one in the laborer's gang," "the dull faced immigrant just landed on the wharf," "the slave at auction." "Why what have you thought yourself?" Whitman asks in "A Song of Occupations,"

> Is it you then that thought yourself less?
> Is it that you thought the President greater than you?
> Or the rich better than you? or the educated wiser
>   than you?

(Because you are greasy or pimpled, or were once
    drunk, or a thief,
Or that you are diseas'd, or rheumatic, or a
    prostitute,
Or from frivolity or impotence, or that you are no
    scholar and never saw your name in print,
Do you give in that you are any less immortal?)

For Walt Whitman, the questions answer themselves. For Walt Whitman, and the religious philosophy which he professes, a principle of inclusivity reigns supreme. And not only does Whitman proclaim a gospel of inclusivity; he places himself within that context, as in "Autumn Rivulets." "Who am I that I should call you more obscene than myself?" he asks of the "felons," the "convicts," the "assassins chain'd and hancuff'd with iron," the "prostitutes flaunting over the trottoirs or obscene in their rooms."

Inside these breast-bones I lie smutch'd and choked,
Beneath this face that appears so impassive hell's
    tides continually run,
Lusts and wickedness are acceptable to me,
I walk with delinquents with passionate love,
I feel I am one of them – I belong to those convicts
    and prostitutes myself,
And henceforth I will not deny them – for how can I
    deny myself?

Walt Whitman does not see himself as better than other people. He knows full well that there is evil in himself, that "hell's tides continually run" in his own being. He knows that he himself, and every other human being is capable of sin, capable of being inhuman, capable of insidious crimes. Walt Whitman knows the truth of the adage which we often proclaim, but also conveniently ignore, "There but for the grace of God go I." And Walt Whitman turns it into a personal affirmation, which though expressed in the first person, is a demand on all selves:

> I feel I am one of them – I belong to those convicts
> and prostitutes myself.

Several decades later, the great Socialist leader, Eugene Debs, who was born in the same year as the publication of the first edition of <u>Leaves of Grass</u>, echoed Whitman's conviction:

> Years ago I recognized my kinship with all living beings, and made up my mind that I was not one bit better than the meanest on earth. I said then, and I say now, that while there is a lower class I am in it, while there is a criminal element I am of it, while there is a soul in prison, I am not free.

Christians, especially evangelical Christians, are fond of saying that John 3:16 is "the gospel in a nutshell." If one were to find Walt Whitman's "gospel in a nutshell," it would have to be these words from "Song of Myself:"

> I speak the pass-word primeval,
> I give the sign of democracy,
> By God! I will accept nothing which all cannot have
> their counterpart of on the same terms.

I do not know the precise significance of what Whitman meant by those powerful phrases, "the password primeval" and the "sign of democracy," but I think I understand their import. The "password primeval" is his "I," the authenticity and the sacredness of the human individual, the authenticity and the sacredness of the self.

The "password primeval" is the individual's recognition of its own inviolable being. "I am." But more than "I am," I belong! I have the right to be here. I have the right to be me. It is in this spirit that Jesse Jackson has disadvantaged young blacks chant "I am Somebody!" The recognition that "I Am Somebody" is essential to a complete humanness.

The "sign of democracy," is the essence of the idea of equality. In a prosaic political sense, it means "one person, one vote." In a democratic sense, it means that kings are not superior to subjects, that presidents are not superior to citizens, that rulers are not superior to the ruled. In a democracy each person is supreme. Whitman's vision is one of absolute equality. Democracy, to Whitman is a sacred institution, and at the heart of democracy is an equality which is necessary for the preservation of liberty.

"By God! I will accept nothing which all cannot have their counterpart of on the same terms," Whitman proclaims, and when Walt Whitman says "all," he means "ALL." He is trying to affirm the conviction that everyone – EVERYONE—owns a fundamental dignity, a fundamental essence, that is measured in terms of equality: the poor as well as the rich; the plain as well as the beautiful; women as well as men; the ruled as well as the rulers; the oppressed as well as the oppressors; the sinner as well as the saint; the bad as well as the good. Beneath all of the divisions we can draw there is an intrinsic quality that belongs to the human being solely because he or she is a human being. It is not something that is earned; it is not something that is granted; it is not something that is gained: it is something that just is, an absolute given.

D

"Each belongs here or anywhere just as much as the well-off, just as much as you," Whitman sings in "I Sing the Body Electric," "Each has his or her place in the procession." The idea of "procession" is a constant, almost mystical, imagery in <u>Leaves of Grass</u>: the universe is in procession; the world and nature is in procession; the whole human family, in time and across time, is in procession. For Walt Whitman everyone has a place in that procession, is an integral and essential part of it. His message is one that needs to be heard and responded to in our day.

Our society and our world needs to find a way to be inclusive, to include all peoples--in their concrete individuality and need --in the human family. One could construct a list out of the modern world, as Whitman did out of his own world: the starving and neglected child; the homeless on the streets of our own cities; the neglected aids victim; the battered and abused woman; the suffering people of the Third World; the disenfranchised people in dictatorships; the oppressed African-Americans in the ghettos of cities; the undocumented aliens – the list could go on and on. Each has a place in the procession. Each has a right to be here. Each has a right to a full and meaningful life. Each has as much claim on the natural resources of the world as anyone else. And we all have the responsibility of helping to bring that kind of world into being. Walt Whitman, in the context of his prophetic vision, presents a challenge to all of us. "Do you know so much yourself that you call the meanest ignorant," he asks in "I Sing the Body Electric,"

> Do you suppose you have a right to a good sight,
> and he or she has no right to a sight?

Do you think matter has cohered together from its
 diffuse float, and the soil is on the surface, and
 water runs and vegetation sprouts,
For you only, and not for him and her?

CHAPTER III
THE FORM COMPLETE

> Behold, the body includes and is the meaning,
> the main concern, and includes and is the soul;
> Whoever you are, how superb and how divine is
>   your body, or any part of it.
>   "Starting from Paumanok"

A

In 1977, NASA, The National Aeronautic and Space Administration, launched two space ships, named Voyager, into outer space. The primary mission of Voyager 1 and 2 was to explore the outer planets in our solar system. Between 1979 and 1981, the two spacecrafts explored Jupiter and Saturn and in the process discovered that there were rings around Jupiter, that there were volcanoes on the Jovian satellite, Io, that both Jupiter and Saturn had more moons than had previously been known, and that the ring system of Saturn was more complex than expected. Between 1986 and 1989, Voyager explored Uranus and Neptune and gave the world both beautiful photographs and greater understanding of those two distant planets.

After their mission to the outer planets the two spacecrafts traveled out of the solar system to wander timelessly, and aimlessly, through the furthest reaches of space.

NASA scientists, realizing that the spacecraft would wander through space for centuries, decided to deal with the possibility that at some point in the future, near or far, those spaceships could be discovered by intelligent beings from worlds other than our own. To this end they decided to put some information about the residents of planet Earth, and about human culture, inside the spacecraft. There were examples of human music, with the hope that music might be some sort of universal language such as was the case in the movie, <u>Close Encounters of the Third Kind</u>. And they made use of mathematics, with the conviction that mathematical laws were uniform all over the universe. One interesting thing they included in the Voyager spacecrafts was a gold plate that contained information about Earth and about the human beings who inhabit it. On this gold plate was a drawing of the solar system to show the location of Earth in relationship to the sun, and pictures of nude human beings: a man; a woman; and a child.

There was some discussion at the time of the launching of the spacecrafts as to whether or not the drawings of the nude human beings should be what we have come to call "anatomically correct:" that is, whether or not the human figures should have genitals. It was decided, if I remember correctly, that the figures should be "anatomically correct," but that decision was not made until after some public discussion of the matter.

If Walt Whitman could have been magically transported, through some time machine, into the later half of the 20th century, he would have both been intrigued and amused by this process. He would have been intrigued because he was always interested in, and quite knowledgeable about, science in general and astronomy in particular. He would have been amused because he could see that the discussion of drawings with genitals was an artifact of the era in which he lived, and a problem that plagued him all of his life. He wrote "anatomically correct" poetry and his world did not much like it.

The year 1855, when Walt Whitman published his first edition of Leaves of Grass, lies right at the heart of what has come to be called the "Victorian Era," with its moral severity, sexual hypocrisy and social stuffiness. It was a time when sexuality was suspect. Any references to sex in art and literature were considered improper and obscene. Sylvester Graham, a temperance reformer and psychological guru of the time, argued that "there had to be something amiss with any organ that sent priority messages to the brain—an erect penis was no more wholesome than a bloated stomach or an infected finger."

"I see through the broadcloth and the gingham," Whitman was to write, and seeing through the "broadcloth and gingham," he could see that the human body, male and female, had organs, including genitals, and functions, including sexuality, which were part and parcel of the whole person. Walt Whitman wanted to put the whole person, including himself, into his poems, and therefore his work had to have an overtly sexual context and content. Leaves of Grass – especially "Song of Myself" and the "Children of Adam" poems – have much vivid and explicit sexual imagery. Whitman describes his sexual agenda in the preface to the 1856 edition of Leaves of Grass, which was dedicated to Ralph Waldo Emerson who, being the Victorian that he was, could not really appreciate its import,

> To me, henceforth, that theory of anything, no matter what, stagnates in its vitals, cowardly and

rotten, while it cannot publicly accept, and publicly name, with specific words, the things on which all existence, all souls, all realization, all decency, all health, all that is worth being here for, all of woman and of man, all beauty, all purity, all sweetness, all friendship, all strength, all life, all immortality depend. The courageous soul, for a year or two to come, may be proved by faith in sex, and by disdaining concessions.

We can understand Whitman a little better on this point, perhaps, if we set his title for his sexual poems, "Children of Adam" over against a line common in the catechisms of the 19th century: "by Adam's fall we sinned all." Adam's fall has, traditionally, been seen in sexual terms. Walt Whitman sees his task as being to redeem Adam in the minds of people, and in redeeming Adam, to redeem the body, and in redeeming the body, to redeem the sexual organs, and in redeeming the sexual organs, to redeem sexuality. "Without shame the man I like knows and avows the deliciousness of his sex," he writes, "Without shame the woman I like knows and avows hers."

We miss the major impact of Whitman's message, however, if we dwell too much on the sexual. It is the whole body, with no part or function deleted, that is of primary interest to Walt Whitman. "I Sing the Body Electric" is a kind of sermon addressed to the life-deniers, the defilers of the body," Edwin Miller writes in <u>Walt Whitman's Poetry, A Psychological Journey</u>:

> The orthodox and the traditionalists delight only in the "beautiful" anatomy of the soul, but Whitman takes "account" of the beauty of every part of the physical anatomy.

B

Whitman's prophetic vision, as has already been suggested, begins with the human self. Walt Whitman sees the self as sacred and divine. But the self which is sacred and divine, for Walt Whitman, is not a disembodied self, it always finds expression in the body. Throughout <u>Leaves of Grass</u> Whitman wrestles with the question of human identity, the question of being, which, in "Song of Myself," he calls the "puzzle of puzzles." What is the real person, he is asking: is it this flesh and blood reality which I experience, or is it something else? There are times when he suggests that it may be something else, but usually he comes down to the conviction that the real person—the real "me"—is what you see, that which lives and moves and loves and feels and knows.

Whitman really is, at heart, a materialist, at least as that word is used in a philosophical sense. "Materialism," in this sense, refers to the idea that physical matter is the only reality. One can see Whitman's "materialism," in his emphasis on "materials" in this selection from "Starting from Paumanok:"

> I will make the poems of materials, for I think they
>   are to be the most spiritual poems,
> And I will make the poems of my body and of
>   immortality,
> For I think I shall then supply myself with the
>   poems of my soul and of immortality.

As usual Walt Whitman speaks of this in term of his own being, in terms of his own body. "If I worship one thing more than another," he says in "Song of Myself," "it shall be the spread of my own body, or any part of it." Whitman obviously delights in his own body, but remember his poetic technique: the reader is to appropriate the "I" and the "my" to themselves and, in the process to celebrate their own bodies and their own beings.

The connections between the body and the self find expression in the very first poem in the final, or standard, edition of <u>Leaves of Grass</u>. The first collection of poems, called "Inscriptions" involves an attempt by Whitman to underscore his agenda, his purpose, in writing his poems. And the very first "Inscription" starts with what Walt Whitman sees as the beginning point for an adequate religious vision for the modern world:

> One's self I sing, a simple separate person,
> Yet utter the word Democratic, the word En-Masse.
>
> Of physiology from top to toe I sing,
> Not physiognomy alone nor brain alone is worthy
>   for the muse,
> I say the Form complete is worthier far,
> The Female equally with the Male I sing.
>
> Of Life immense in passion pulse, and power,
> Cheerful, for freest action form'd under the laws
>   divine,
> The Modern Man I sing.

Whitman's use of the words "physiology" and "physiognomy" in this passage provides a fundamental clue to Whitman's thought. According to the <u>American Heritage Dictionary</u>, "physiology" refers to "the essential and characteristic life processes, activities, and functions...of an organism." "Physiognomy" is defined as "the art of judging human character by facial qualities" or "aspect or character of an inanimate or abstract entity." Whitman is interested in physical reality. He is not interested in appearances. It is the totality of the human self, as it is defined in terms of the whole body, "the form complete," that interests Whitman. "the unseen is proved by the seen," Whitman avows, "If anything is sacred, the human body is sacred."

C

"If anything is sacred the human body is sacred," Whitman says, and by that he means the entire body, with all of its constituent parts, and with all of its numerous functions. Whitman's idea of the sacredness of the body, of "the form complete," not only includes the body as a whole but every "tag and part" of it. "I will not make poems with reference to parts," Whitman says in "Starting from Paumanok," "but I will make poems, songs, thoughts, with reference to ensemble."

It is the body as ensemble, the body with all of its constituent parts as part of the whole, which is sacred to Whitman. "O my body! I dare not desert the likes of you in other men and women, nor the likes of the parts of you," Whitman says in "Children of Adam." He then goes on to name dozens and dozens of the parts of the human body – eyebrows, roof of the mouth, wrist joints, hips, toes, manballs, nipples etc. – "All attitudes, all the shapeliness, all the belongings of my or your body or of any one's body, male and female" – and then concludes:

> O I say these are not the parts and poems of the
>   body only, but of the soul,
> O I say now these are the soul!

This theme of the sacredness of a body which incorporates in its sacredness all of the parts of the body, and which finds its most extensive expression in "Children of Adam," also was powerfully expressed in "Song of Myself" with words many people have, and still do find offensive:

> Through me forbidden voices,
> Voices of sexes and lusts, voices veil'd and I remove the veil,
> Voices indecent by me clarified and transfigur'd.
>
> I do not press my fingers across my mouth,
> I keep as delicate around the bowels as around the head and heart,
> Divine am I inside and out, and I make holy whatever I touch or am touched from,
> The scent of these arm-pits aroma finer than prayer,
> This head more than churches, bibles, and all creeds....

One can readily understand those who see a kind of crudeness in expressions like "the scent of these arm pits finer than prayer," and "I keep as delicate around the bowels as around the head and heart." But one can also readily understand, after a moment of thought, that it is this very crudity which best serves Whitman's poetic, and programmatic purposes. His principle of concreteness seems almost to demand it. To perspire is part of what it means to be human, for example, and if the human body is sacred, then to perspire must have aspects of the sacred. The bowels are as important a part of the body as the head is and therefore both must be sacred. Whitman lived in a world where to mention such things, and to mention certain parts of the body, or to mention certain bodily functions, was deemed taboo, and he considered it an important function of his prophetic mission, as he put it, "to remove the veil," and to make sure that "voices" once considered "indecent" are "clarifi'd and transfigur'd:"

> Welcome is every organ and attribute of me, and of any man hearty and clean,
> Not an inch or a particle of an inch is vice, and none shall be less familiar than the rest.

"And if the body does not do as much as the soul?" Whitman asks, "And if the body were not the soul, what is the soul?" The word "soul" and the world "body" often seem interchangeable with Whitman and it is apparently part of his program to merge them into one entity. "It is Whitman's creed of the equality of the body and the soul," notes Karl Shapiro in Start With The Sun.

> The body is not cursed; it is the miraculous materialization of the soul.... I do not think for a second that Whitman was either narcissistic or egomaniac; he was trying to obliterate the fatal dualism of body and soul.

For Whitman, the soul and the body are one. That idea of the merging of the soul with the body, though quite common today, was rare in 19th century America. Sidney Lanier, 19th century poet, concluded an essay on Whitman with these words,

> I cannot close these hasty words upon the Whitman school without a fervent protest, in the name of all art and all artists, against a poetry which has painted a great scrawling picture of the human body, and has written under it: "This is the soul."

But that is exactly what Whitman did, and what he intended to do. And he was, perhaps, the first American literary figure to do so. D.H. Lawrence captures this aspect of Whitman's prophetic vision in insightful words:

> [Whitman] was the first to smash the old moral conception that the soul of man is something "superior" and "above" the flesh. Even Emerson still maintained this tiresome "superiority" of the soul. Even Melville could not get over it. Whitman was the first heroic seer to seize the soul by the scruff of her neck and plant her down among the potsherds.
>
> "There!" he said to the soul. "Stay there!"
>
> Stay there. Stay in the flesh. Stay in the limbs and in the lips and in the belly. Stay in the breast and womb. Stay there, O soul, where you belong. Stay in the dark limbs of Negroes. Stay in the body of the prostitute. Stay in the sick flesh of the syphilitic. Stay in the marsh where the calamus grows. Stay there, soul, where you belong.

E

Whitman uses three different words to express individual human existence: self, soul, body; and he often uses them somewhat interchangeably. The reader can easily be confused with such changes, especially when, as is sometimes the case, Whitman himself does not appear to know just exactly what he means. The reader cannot be too far off the mark, however, if he or she takes the self to be the result of a merger, or a fusion, of the soul and the body.

The substantial reality which results from that merger, Whitman refers to as a "knit of identity."

At any rate, the self, the "I" that is central to Walt Whitman's prophetic vision, is not an abstraction. It finds expression through the body. A religion appropriate for the modern world has to accept that body, Whitman felt, and proclaim its divinity, as Whitman says in "Starting from Paumanok:"

> Behold, the body includes and is the meaning, the
>   main concern, and includes and is the soul
> Whoever you are, how superb and how divine is
>   your body, or any part of it.

With that thought in mind we can conclude by returning with Whitman's Adam to his Garden of Eden:

> As Adam early in the morning,
> Walking forth from the bower refresh'd with sleep,
> Behold me where I pass, hear my voice, approach,
> Touch me, touch the palm of your hand to my body
>   as I pass,
> Be not afraid of my body.

CHAPTER IV
ALL WERE LACKING, IF SEX WERE LACKING

> A Woman waits for me, she contains all, nothing is lacking,
> Yet all were lacking if sex were lacking, or if the moisture of the right man were lacking.
> "A Woman Waits For Me"

A

Five years after the publication of the first edition of Leaves of Grass, Whitman was ready to publish his third edition. This time he had secured a publisher, and Whitman spent a few weeks in Boston to oversee the printing and production. During this time he had several opportunities to talk with Ralph Waldo Emerson, who had lavishly praised the first edition of Leaves of Grass:

> I find it the most extraordinary piece of wit and wisdom that America has yet contributed. I greet you at the beginning of a great career.

On one of those occasions – and I think it to be one of the most important and interesting moments in the history of American literature – the two poets walked in Boston

Commons and talked about whether not Whitman should expunge certain sexual references from his work. Emerson felt that Whitman should delete the overt sexual references, not because he himself objected to them, but because their inclusion would prevent the poet from receiving, in a puritan time, a fair hearing, and would, as well, diminish the financial success of the book.

For two hours they walked back and forth through the commons, with Emerson presenting his case. We do not know exactly what took place in that conversation, but we can imagine Emerson arguing that the world was not ready for a literature that named genital organs and dealt frankly with sex and with intercourse. We can imagine Emerson telling the new poet that he had a lot of valuable things to say and should not jeopardize his chances of becoming a successful poet by affronting the staid sensibilities of the nation. After he had presented his arguments, however they were phrased, he turned to Whitman and asked, "What have you to say to such things?" Whitman replied, "Only that while I cannot answer at all, I feel more settled than ever to adhere to my own theory." Where upon the two men went to the American House, a Boston landmark, and had a "good dinner." They went to the American House, because Mrs. Emerson would not permit Waldo to bring Whitman, whom she considered a reprobate, into her house.

Because he refused to listen to Emerson's realistic advice, Whitman was to spend his whole life seeking a "fair hearing." And yet Whitman felt, from the perspective of his own "theory," that he had no choice in the matter. The sexual poems were intrinsic to his prophetic vision. In his later years he talked to his friend Horace Traubel about that conversation with Emerson.

"When I tried to take those pieces out of the scheme the whole scheme came down upon my ears," he said of Emerson's advice,

> He did not see the significance of the sex element as I had put it into the book and resolutely there stuck to it – he did not see that if I had cut sex out I might just as well have cut everything out – the full scheme would no longer exist – it would have been violated in its most sensitive spot.

James E. Miller, writing in <u>Start With The Sun</u>, agrees:

> If by some intricate method the sexual content of <u>Leaves of Grass</u> were to be expunged, the book would be maimed and impotent before us, its strength and vitality obliterated. As well castrate a man as bowdlerize <u>Leaves of Grass</u>.

B

The very first line in the "Children of Adam" collection is "To The Garden Anew Ascending." Whitman's purpose in these poems involves a retelling of the story of Adam and Eve in the Garden of Eden. In the original Garden of Eden – and I am sure most people remember the story – Eve ate of the fruit of the tree of knowledge and persuaded Adam to eat as well. Once having eaten they discovered their own nakedness and covered their nakedness with leaves. Because of this they were expelled from the Garden of Eden. In Christian accounts of the story, still further, this experience is seen as "the fall;" the fall from grace. And because of their sins people need the saving sacrifice of Jesus Christ.

Now, one common interpretation of this story is that Adam and Eve discovered their own genitals, discovered their own sexuality, and were ashamed. The echo of that shame resounds down through all of Judeo-Christian history. There is something nasty about sex, something evil, even. You may remember that St. Paul said it was all right for Christians to marry, but not because that was an intrinsic good in itself, but because it was "better to marry than to burn." It would be better not to have a sex drive, but since we do it is better to get things over with as soon as possible. There is a strong element of shame which runs through our entire culture, an element of shame that has its roots in the traditional Garden of Eden story.

In Walt Whitman's Garden of Eden it is an entirely different story. It starts at the same place, with Adam and Eve discovering their own nakedness, discovering their own bodies, discovering their own genitals, discovering their own sexuality. But instead of being ashamed they delight in it, they revel in it "Without shame the man I like knows and avows the deliciousness of his own sex, without shame the woman I like knows and avows the deliciousness of hers." They know that in dealing with their bodies and in dealing with sexuality, they are dealing with their most fundamental and authentic selves.

In the "Children of Adam" poems Whitman celebrates three aspects of sexuality, and refers to them again and again: the sexual drive, "the divine madness," "the muscular urge;" sexual intercourse, "the blending," the "act-poem of eyes, hands, hips and bosoms;" and the magic of procreation. People of every land and time have shared in this need to express their sexuality, the need to blend and to merge with another human being, the need to connect ourselves both to the past and to the future by a process of procreation that brought us into being and extends ourselves into the infinite future. For Whitman a religion that is universal has to begin with our most fundamental and basic attributes: our bodies and our sexuality. They are their own reasons for being. They need no justification. As Whitman asks in "I Sing the Body Electric,"

> Have you ever loved the body of a woman?
> Have you ever loved the body of a man?
> Do you not see that these are exactly the same to all
>   in all nations and times all over the earth?

C

"I am he that aches with amorous love," Whitman writes in "From Pent-up Aching Rivers,"

> From what of myself without which I were nothing,
> From what I am determin'd to make illustrious even
>   if I stand sole among men,
>
> From my own voice resonant, singing the phallus,
> Singing the song of procreation,
> Singing the need of superb children and therein
>   superb grown people,
> Singing the muscular urge and the blending,
>
> Singing the bedfellow's song, (O resistless
>   yearning!
> O for any and each the body correlative attracting!
> O for you whoever you are your correlative body!
> O it, more than all else, you delighting!)

Whitman writes about the "hungry gnaw that eats me night and day," about the "Mystic deliria, the madness amorous, the utter abandonment" of sexual passion:

> The furious storm through me careening, I passionately trembling,
> The oath of the inseperableness of two together, of the woman that loves me and whom I love more than my life, that oath swearing,
> (O I willingly stake all for you,
> O let me be lost if it must be so!
> O you and I! What is it to us what the rest do or think?
> What is all else to us? Only that we enjoy each other and exhaust each other if it must be so;)

And Whitman describes, in some detail, the physical aspects of lovemaking, the physical reality of sexual intercourse:

> Limitless limpid jets of love hot and enormous, quivering jelly of love, white-blow and delirious juice,
> Bridegroom night of love working surely and softly into the prostrate dawn,
> Lost in the cleave of the clasping and sweet-flesh'd day.

The songs in "Children of Adam" are songs of lust. "Through me forbidden voices, Voices of sexes and lusts, voices veil'd and I remove the veil, Voices indecent by me clarified and transfigur'd," he says in "Song of Myself," "I believe in the flesh and the appetites, Seeing, hearing, feeling, are miracles, and each part and tag of me is a miracle." But if these are songs of lust these are also songs of human love, and human longing, and human intimacy:

> Once I pass'd through a populous city imprinting my brain for future use, with all its shows, architecture, customs, traditions,
> Yet now of all that city I remember only a woman I casually met there who detain'd me for love of me,
> Day by day and night by night we were together – all else has long been forgotten by me,
> I remember I say only that woman who passionately clung to me,
> Again we wander, we love, we separate again,
> Again she holds me by the hand, I must not go,
> I see her close beside me with silent lips sad and tremulous.

The "Children of Adam" poems contain intimations of his "theory" as well, intimations of why sex is so important, of why he could not heed Emerson's advice. "A Woman Waits for Me, she contains all, nothing is lacking, Yet all were lacking if sex were lacking, or if the moisture of the right man were lacking," he writes:

> Sex contains all, bodies, souls, meanings, proofs, purities, delicacies, results, promulgations,
> Songs, commands, health, pride, the maternal mystery, the seminal milk,
> All hopes, benefactions, bestowals, all the passions, loves, beauties, delights of the earth,
> All the governments, judges, gods, follow'd persons of the earth,
> These are contained in sex as parts of itself and justifications of itself.

D

Most students of Walt Whitman have noticed a woodenness, or an artificial quality in the "Children of Adam" poems. These poems do not seem to have the passion and the feeling that the "Calamus" poems do. They do not sound like they are the love poems of a lover. There does appear to be a lot of truth to such observations, and yet several women, in his century, and because of his poetry, did find Walt Whitman and his poems passionately sexual. Women easily fell in love with Whitman both as a poet and as a man and there was more than one woman who, after reading his poems, decided that she was destined to be his lover. The most interesting of these situations involved Anne Gilchrist.

Anne Gilchrist was a rather prominent English literary figure of the time who was a confidant of the Rossetti circle in England, and who was a personal friend of both Alfred Lord Tennyson and Thomas Carlyle. It was William Michael Rossetti who had introduced <u>Leaves of Grass</u> to England, in a collection of poems that did not include the more overtly sexual ones. Rossetti gave a copy of this abridged collection to Anne Gilchrist and encouraged her to write a review of the book from a woman's perspective. Her review, "An English Woman's Estimate of Walt Whitman," was published first in England and then in America. <u>Leaves of Grass</u> is "a perfectly fearless, candid ennobling treatment of the life of the body," she wrote, and from it I learned for the first time "what love meant...what life meant." "I know that poetry must do one of two things," she added,

> either own this man as equal with her highest, completest manifestors, or stand aside, and admit

that there is something come into the world nobler, diviner than herself, one that is free of the universe, and can tell its secrets as none before.

Happy America, that he should be her son! One sees, indeed, that only a young giant of a nation could produce this kind of greatness, so full of ardor, the elasticity, the inexhaustible vigor and freshness, their joyousness, the audacity of youth.

Anne Gilchrist admired <u>Leaves of Grass</u> a great deal, as you can tell from these remarks, but more than that she fell madly in love with the author of the words. It was as if Whitman was speaking directly to her and of his love for her. After the publication of her review, Whitman sent her a copy of the latest edition of <u>Leaves of Grass</u>, through Rossetti, and did not include a personal note to her, and that crushed her. "I was so sure you would speak, would send me some sign," she wrote to Whitman, much later, "O surely in the ineffable tenderness of thy look speaks the yearning of thy man-soul toward my woman soul." Whitman did not respond to this letter, either.

Still receiving no sign, Anne Gilchrist decided time was too valuable to waste. So, in 1871, a few months after the appearance of her literary review, with Walt at age 50, she went out in the country, to a field that was a favorite spot of hers, and wrote Walt Whitman a love letter, the writing of which, she said, made her feel "relieved, joyful, buoyant once more." "Dear Walt, it clings so close, so close to the Soul and Body, all so tenderly dear, so beautiful, so sacred," she wrote,

> it yearns with such passion to soothe and comfort & fill thee with tender joy; it aspires as grandly, as

gloriously as thy own soul, soft & tender to nestle and caress. If God were to say to me—see—"he that you love you shall not be given to in this life—he is going to sail on the unknown sea—will you go with him?" –never yet has a bride sprung into her husbands arms with the joy I would take thy hand & spring from the shore.

Now these letters "scared the hell" out of Walt Whitman, but after a time he decided he had to respond. In his letter which was as Justin Kaplan put it, "guarded and deliberate," Whitman says that he is not "insensitive to your love," but that "My book is my best letter, my response, my truest explanation of all. In it I have put my body & spirit." And then concludes:

> Enough that there surely exists between us so beautiful & delicate a relation, accepted by both of us with joy.

The word "enough" in that last sentence, crushed her, Anne Gilchrist said, in response to his letter – it was "like a blow in the breast to me." But she had decided after studying the letter that her love had not been rejected, but only that the consummation of it had been deferred. "You might not be able to give me your great love yet," she replied, "but I can wait."

For a year and a half letters like this crossed the Atlantic, and all the time the passion expressed by them continued to scare Whitman. Finally he felt he had to be more direct:

> Let me warn you somewhat about myself – and yourself also. You must not construct such an unauthorized and imaginary ideal figure and call it

W.W. and so devotedly invest your loving nature in it. The actual W.W. is a very plain personage, and entirely unworthy of such devotion.

Even this protestation did not deter Anne Gilchrist, however. Over his protestations she determined to bring her children and come to America to be near him. And she did. In 1876 she moved to Philadelphia, just across the river from Camden, and lived there for two years. She and Walt became good friends – he frequently took the ferry across the river to have lunch or tea, or dinner with her --- but almost certainly, they never became lovers, and she never bore a child of his which was her earnest desire. Anne Gilchrist moved back to England in 1878, and died in 1885. In one of the poems in Leaves of Grass, written on the occasion of her death, Whitman calls Anne Gilchrist his "greatest woman friend."

I treat this matter at some length because there is so much feeling, among students of Whitman, that the "Children of Adam" poems lack emotional strength, that the poems are deficient in personal passion and seem to deal with sex as theory rather than sex as content. But the response of Anne Gilchrist, and other women, to the "Children of Adam" motif in Leaves of Grass, amply demonstrates that they do, or at least did, have a power – an erotic and sexual power – all their own. The poet could reach out through his poems and actually become seductive.

E

In his preface to the second edition of Leaves of Grass, the edition which contained the laudatory letter from Emerson and which was dedicated to Emerson, Whitman talks about his sexual agenda:

> ...the body of a man or woman...is so far quite unexpressed in poems....Of bards for These States, if it comes to a question, it is whether they shall celebrate in poems the eternal decency of the amativeness of Nature, the motherhood of all, or whether they shall be the bards of the fashionable delusion of the inherent nastiness of sex, and of the feeble and querulous modesty of deprivation.
>
> Infidelism usurps most with foetid face; among the rest infidelism about sex. By silence or obedience the pens of savans, poets, historians, biographers, and the rest have long connived at the filthy law...that what makes the manhood of a man, that sex, womanhood, maternity, desires, lusty animations, organs, acts, are unmentionable and to be ashamed of.... This filthy law has to be repealed...Of women just as much as man, it is the interest that there should not be infidelism about sex, but perfect faith.

The "fashionable delusion of the inherent nastiness of sex," and "the feeble and querulous modesty of deprivation," were, in many ways, characteristic of American literature before the time of Whitman. Even Emerson could not bring himself to deal with the human body or to deal, in other than romantic ways, with human sexuality. Walt Whitman deserves credit, more than any other literary figure in our national history, for making the human body and human sexuality an appropriate subject for literary efforts. He may have been clumsy, he may have been wooden, in his treatment of sex, but he was the first person in American literature to treat it at all. Whitman, as Ezra Pound put it in a poem addressed to Walt Whitman, "broke the new wood." It was Walt Whitman who laid the groundwork for future poets who could unite love and sex.

That "fashionable delusion of the inherent nastiness of sex," as reflected in early American literature, furthermore, derives from an attitude that is endemic, as well, in the dominant religious expression of our culture –the Judeo-Christian tradition. The main import of the "Children of Adam" poems is an impassioned rejection of what he saw as a main theme in the dominant cultural religion. It may well be, as Rollo May says in Love and Will, that the Victorian world wanted "love, without sex," and the modern world wants "sex without love." Whitman would have dismissed both of these perspectives. But in his world, the Victorian world, sex itself was seen as somehow impure. Whitman chooses his words carefully and his use of the word "foetid" –fetid—in the previous quotation well expresses his feelings. The word "fetid" means, "having an offensive odor, foul-smelling." In his world there was something "offensive," something "foul-smelling," about human sexuality, and his task as a prophetic poet and the task of all "true poets," is to condemn that perspective. Whitman refers to that perspective as a "filthy law," and condemns the literature of his time because by "silence" literary figures have "connived" in enforcing this "filthy law."

Literary people, especially American literary people, had not, before the time of Whitman, insisted that sex was a proper subject for literature. But it is not only literary concerns Whitman is here dealing with, it is also religious concerns. "Infidelism" is a religious word, and the literary world, the nation, and the religious culture, have exhibited an "infidelism about sex." "The filthy law, has to be repealed," the poet/prophet thunders, "there should not be infidelism about sex, but perfect faith." For Walt Whitman, sex has to be seen, absolutely, as sacred. It must be seen as part of an unfolding process: if the self is sacred then the body is sacred; if the body is sacred, then the parts and functions of the body are sacred; if the functions of the body are sacred, then sexuality – the sex drive, the physical act of intercourse, the processes of reproduction – all partake of the sacred. "The quivering fire that plays through" the human body, Whitman insists, "has reasons, most wondrous."

"Sex contains all," Walt Whitman says in "Children of Adam," "all were lacking if sex were lacking." "All" is an absolute word, and Whitman is clearly trying to express an absolute conviction. Central to his prophetic vision – so central that the whole structure would fall apart without it – is the total acceptance of human sexuality. I would guess that this conviction springs from the realization that the "self" which he celebrates, and which is the prototype of all other "selves," – the self which is the merger or fusion of the "soul" and the "body" – would not have "being," would not have "identity," if it were not, in fact, possible through the sexual behavior, and sexual processes, of human beings. The identification of sex with procreation is, therefore, a common theme in <u>Leaves of Grass</u>.

One fails entirely in reading Walt Whitman, however, if one thinks of him as seeing sexuality as having totally to do with reproduction. The physical pleasures of sex, the warmth and the closeness that sexuality brings to human beings, the ecstasy which it can produce, are all intrinsic parts of his prophetic vision. "Children of Adam" contains many poems celebrating, rather graphically, the physical nature of sexuality, but it also contains the love, the warmth, the togetherness which sexuality brings into the hearts and the lives of people:

I have perceiv'd that to be with those I like is enough,
To stop in company with the rest at evening is enough,
To be surrounded by beautiful, curious, breathing, laughing flesh is enough,
To pass among them or touch any one, or rest my arm ever so lightly round his or her neck for a moment, what is this then?

I do not ask any more delight, I swim in it as in a sea.
There is something in staying close to men and women and looking on them, and in the contact and odor of them, that pleases the soul well,
All things please the soul, but these please the soul well.

CHAPTER V
CAROLS FOR COMRADES AND LOVERS

> It seems to me there are other men in other lands
>   yearning and thoughtful,
> And it seems to me if I could know those men I
>   should become attached to them as I do to men
>   in my own lands,
> O I know we should be brethren and lovers,
>   "This Moment Yearning and Thoughtful"

A

Phrenology was a pseudo science of the nineteenth century that claimed to be able to tell about the personality of people by studying the shape of individual human skulls. Practitioners of phrenology would come up with a chart showing the strong and weak characteristics of a client by reading the bumps on the head. Whitman became very enamored of phrenology when he was a young man, had his bumps read in July 1849 at the Fowler and Wells Phrenological Cabinet in New York City, and was always somewhat proud of the personality profile that resulted. Whitman was not alone in this. Phrenology, for a time, was a very popular idea among the literate and educated classes.

Lorenzo Fowler, who did the phrenological examination of Walt Whitman, found his patient to be adequately endowed in all of the categories of the chart and to be superior in three areas: "amativeness" (sexual love); "philoprogenitiveness" (love of humanity) and "adhesiveness" (male friendship). Fowler, in his written analysis of his examination had this to say,

> This man has a grand physical constitution, and power to live to a good old age. He is undoubtedly descended from the soundest and hardiest stock. Size of head large. Leading traits of character appear to be Friendship, Sympathy, Sublimity, and Self-esteem, and markedly among his combination the dangerous faults of Indolence, a tendency to the pleasures of Voluptuousness [which I presume means love of pleasure] and Alimentiveness [which I presume means love of eating] and a certain reckless swing of animal will, too unmindful, probably, of the conviction of others.

Whitman loved this report on his character, thought it represented who he really was, and preserved his "chart of bumps" to the end of his days. Although he realized, as time went on, that phrenology was not valid science after all, he remained attached to the language of phrenology because it provided him with some important ideas for Leaves of Grass. Especially was this so in helping him to understand the nature of love.

In the phrenological scheme there were two personality traits that related to personal and intimate love: amativeness and adhesiveness. Amativeness is derived from a Latin word which means "to love," has the same roots as does the word "amorous," involves love between man and woman, and includes sexual desire, sexual intercourse, and procreation. "Adhesiveness," which is derived from the Latin word, "adhere," and which can, in turn, lead to such thoughts as "sticking together" and "attachment," involves, according to my dictionary, "physical attraction or joining of two substances." The phrenological categories of "amativeness" and "adhesiveness" gave Walt Whitman the idea for his two collections of love poems. "Amativeness," sexual love, found expression in the "Children of Adam" poems. "Adhesiveness," male friendship, found expression in the "Calamus" poems.

Walt Whitman's symbol for his poems of "manly love" is a grassy plant which is also called "sweet flag." Whitman explained his use of the symbol for these poems in a letter to M.D. Conway in November 1867:

> "Calamus" is a common word here; it is the very large and aromatic grass, or root, spears three feet high – often called "sweet flag" – grows all over the Northern and Middles States...The recherché or ethereal sense, as used in my book, arises probably from it, Calamus presenting the biggest and hardiest kind of spears of grass, and from its fresh, aromatic, pungent bouquet.

There is also a sexual image in the calamus plant, especially in the calamus root, which at times is pink and looks something like an erect penis. Whitman uses this imagery, in "Song of Myself," when he refers to his own genitals as "root of wash'd sweet flag! Timorous pond-snipe! Nest of guarded duplicate eggs." One can gather from this that the "Calamus" poems are poems about love between men – hardy men who are proud of their male bodies, and are knitted together by a bond of comradeship.

It is interesting to note, however, that the phrenological symbol for "adhesiveness" – and the phrenologists had a symbol for every personality trait – was two women embracing. Whitman's "Calamus" poems are masculine and do celebrate love between men. There is imagery here that can suggest what we have come to call, in our day, "same sex" love.

Walt Whitman, as always, starts with his own concrete self. He is a man. The images found in "Calamus" are masculine, but, especially when one considers Whitman's sexual egalitarianism, the "adhesive" poems in "Calamus" can be seen as celebrating intimate and warm relationships between people of the same sex as the "amativeness" in "Children of Adam" celebrate intimate and warm relationships between people of the opposite sex. Walt Whitman saw himself, the poet/prophet, before anything else, as a great lover and the champion of love between human beings:

> Records ages hence,
> Come, I will take you down underneath this impassive exterior, I will tell you what to say of me,
> Publish my name and hang up my picture as that of the tenderest lover,
> The friend the lover's portrait, of whom his friend his lover was fondest,
> Who was not proud of his songs, but of the measureless ocean of love within him, and freely pour'd it forth.

B

The "Calamus" poems are a celebration of intimate human relationships; a celebration of the relationship between "Comrades and Lovers." In these poems, Whitman is singing, as he says, "In Spring Collect For Lovers." He sees such songs, and the act of singing them, as an important aspect of his prophetic vision: "For who but I should understand lovers and all their sorrow and joy? Who but I should be the poet of comrades?" There is a pervasive intimacy all through the "Calamus" poems: scenes of human affection between men; men embracing; men hugging; men kissing. There is a powerful physical and psychological and sexual quality to such intimacy:

> O you whom I often and silently come where you
>   are that I may be with you,
> As I walk by your side or sit near, or remain in the
>   same room with you,
> Little you know the subtle electric fire that for your
>   sake is playing within me.

Walt Whitman longs for a time when such signs of affection will be normative in human society: "I wish to infuse myself upon you til I see it common for you to walk hand in hand." In "What Think You I take My Pen In Hand?" Whitman asks what the reader thinks he is "to record?" The "majestic" battle ship that he saw "under full sail?" "The splendors of the past day," or "of the night?" or how about "The vaunted glory and growth of the great city spread around me?" No, the hero of this poem says, not those,

> But merely of two simple men I saw to-day on the pier in the midst of the crowd, parting the parting of dear friends,
> The one to remain hung on the other's neck and passionately kiss'd him
> While the other to depart tightly prest the one to remain in his arms.

One senses in this scene on the pier, both the "sorrow and joy" of comrades and lovers. There is the joy of relatedness and there is the sorrow of loneliness. Leaves of Grass is a lonely book. But it is a book written to overcome loneliness by establishing intimate contacts. It is a book written to deal with the longing of the human heart for love and comradeship. The "I" in Whitman's poems are always, as I have mentioned previously, of a two-fold nature. There is the "first person singular" and there is the "I" of the reader. When Whitman writes "I," it is Walt Whitman speaking but when the reader reads "I" the reader becomes the "I," or must become the "I," to capture the essence of the poem. Every human being needs to find a place in another person's world. Whitman understood this and in his Calamus poems tried to deal with it. "Calamus" is about the "I" – Whitman's "I" and the readers "I" – finding place in another person's world.

Before Whitman settled on the name "Calamus" to define his "adhesiveness" poems, he called the collection "Live Oak, with Moss." This suggests that one of his most beautiful poems, "I Saw in Louisiana A Live Oak Growing," may provide the theme for the collection. Many people, including Mark Van Doren, have suggested that the only true love poems in Leaves of Grass are found in "Calamus," and if that is the case, this poem may be the most beautiful love poem of all. In the poem the poet describes a live-oak he saw growing in Louisiana, "all alone stood it and the moss hung down from the branches, without any companion it grew there uttering joyous leaves of dark green." In the poem he muses on that tree, thinks of his own dear friends, and of what they mean to him, and then concludes,

> For all that, and though the live-oak glistens there in Louisiana solitary in a wide flat space,
> Uttering joyous leaves all its life without a Friend a lover near,
> I know very well I could not.

C

At its most intimate level, the "Calamus" poems are an attempt to overcome separateness, and to break out of loneliness into the warmth of loving relationships. But the intimacy which Whitman envisions is not only personal, in the specific sense of contact between two human beings struggling to overcome loneliness: he thinks of such intimacy as being normative for his vision of a just and democratic society. He wants to establish a community of comrades, a nation of comrades. In that community of comrades, "the city of friends,"

> Nothing was greater there than the quality of robust love, it led the rest,
> It was seen every hour in the actions of the men of that city,
> And in all their looks and words.

That vision moves on from the community to the nation. In "For You, O Democracy," Whitman sings, "Come, I will make the continent indissoluble,"

> I will plant companionship thick as trees along all
>   the rivers of America, and along the shores of
>   the great lakes, and all over the prairies,
> I will make inseparable cities with their arms about
>   each other's necks,
>   By the love of comrades,
>   By the manly love of comrades.

Ultimately that vision of "comrades and lovers" goes on to embrace the whole world. "This moment yearning and thoughtful sitting alone," he sings, "It seems to me there are other men in other lands yearning and thoughtful," – "in Germany, Italy, France, Spain, or far, far away, in China, or in Russia or Japan, talking other dialects," – and he wants to establish the relationship of love and comradeship with them all:

> It seems to me if I could know those men I should
>   become attached to them as I do to men in my
>   own lands,
> O I know we should be brethren and lovers,
> I know I should be happy with them.

The prophetic vision of a human community of lovers transcends locality and nation and nationality to embrace the whole world, but it also moves beyond that to cross the boundaries of time. It becomes for Whitman a uniting force for humanity, for people on a "Perpetual Journey" – a force that conquers even death. In "On the Terrible Doubt of Appearances," he deals with metaphysical questions. What if "identify beyond the grave is a beautiful fable only?" he asks, what if the "things I perceive...are only apparitions." What if the world is but an illusion? He muses on such questions and then responds with his affirmation,

> To me these and the like of these are curiously
>   answer'd by my lovers, my dear friends,
> When he whom I love travels with me or sits a long
>   while holding me by the hand,
> When the subtle air, the impalpable, the sense that
>   words and reason hold not, surround us and
>   pervade us.
> Then I am charged with untold and untellable
>   wisdom, I am silent, I require nothing further.
> I cannot answer the question of appearances or that
>   of identity beyond the grave.
> But I walk or sit indifferent, I am satisfied,
> He ahold of my hand has completely satisfied me.

Walt Whitman's vision of lovers and of comrades transcends death, and makes lovers and comrades of those who have gone on before and shall follow after. I can feel this is my own being because I love Whitman, and because I see him as one of my lovers and comrades. He speaks to me, across a century now, through his poems and through his ideas. It is almost as if he were speaking to me when he wrote, more than a century ago, the concluding words of Calamus,

> Full of life now, compact, visible,
> I, forty years old the eighty-third year of the States,
> To one a century hence or any number of centuries
>   hence,
> To you yet unborn these, seeking you.
>
> When you read these I that was visible am become
>   invisible,
> Now it is you, compact, visible, realizing my
>   poems, seeking me,

> Fancying how happy you were if I could be with you and become your comrade;
> Be it as if I were with you. (Be not too certain but I am now with you.)

D

John Addington Symonds was an English literary scholar who had discovered Walt Whitman while a student at Trinity College, Cambridge. Leaves of Grass, he was to say, "revolutionized my previous conceptions, and made another man of me." Symonds, who was married, and the father of a couple of children, was also, by nature, homosexual and he felt that he could read into the "Calamus" poems a validation of homosexual love.

Over the span of two decades he wrote many letters to Whitman about the "Calamus" poems, seeking to understand their underlying nature. "I desire to hear from your own lips – or from your pen – some story of athletic friendship from which to learn the truth," he wrote in one letter,

> What the love of man for man has been in the past I think I know. What it is here now, I know – alas! What you say it can and shall be I dimly discern in your poems. But this hardly satisfies me – so desirous as I am of learning what you teach. Some day, perhaps – in some form I know not what, but in your own chosen form – you will tell me more about the Love of Friends! Till then I wait. Meanwhile you have told me more than anyone beside.

In another, somewhat more direct, letter he wrote:

> In your conception of Comradeship, do you contemplate the possible intrusion of those semi-sexual emotions and actions which no doubt do occur between men? I do not ask whether you approve of them, or regard them as a necessary part of this relation? But I should much like to know whether you are prepared to leave them to the inclinations and the conscience of the individuals concerned...I agree with the objections I have mentioned that, human nature being what it is, and some men having a strong natural bias towards persons of their own sex, the enthusiasms of "Calamus" is calculated to encourage ardent and physical intimacies. But I do not agree with them in thinking such a result would absolutely be prejudicial to social interests.

Do the "Calamus" poems encourage homosexual love? Is it their intention to encourage, between people of the same sex, "ardent and physical intimacies?" That is what John Addington Symonds wanted to know. In a sense, like Anne Gilchrist, Symonds felt that the poet was talking to him: not in the intimate personal sense, which characterized Gilchrist's feelings, but as if speaking to his homosexuality. The poet seemed to be affirming what Symonds, himself, felt.

The correspondence with John Addington Symonds, like those love letters of Anne Gilchrist, however, scared the hell out of Walt Whitman. And like the Gilchrist affair, there came a point where Whitman felt he had to respond. So, in 1890, when he was 71 years of age, Whitman wrote Symonds a letter, a rather angry letter.

"Ab't the questions on Calamus pieces &c: they quite daze me," he wrote,

> L of G is only to be rightly construed by and within its own atmosphere and essential character – all of its pages & pieces so coming strictly under that – that the Calamus part has even allow'd the possibility of such construction as mention'd is terrible – I am fain to hope the pages themselves are not to be even mention'd for such gratuitous and quite at the time entirely undream'd & unreck'd possibility of morbid inferences –wh' are disavow'd by me & seem damnable. Then one great difference between you and me, temperament & theory, is restraint – I know that while I have a horror of ranting & brawling I at certain moments let the spirit impulse, (?demon) rage its utmost, its wildest, damndest – (I feel to do so in my L of G & I do). I end the matter by saying I wholly stand by L of G as it is, long as all parts and pages are construed as I said by their own ensemble, spirit & atmosphere.

Whitman went on, in this letter, to talk about his poor health, and concludes with an amazing and incredible statement,

> Tho' always unmarried I have had six children – two are dead – one living southern grandchild, fine boy who writes to me occasionally. Circumstances connected with their benefit and fortune have separated me from intimate relations.

Now, I say that this statement is "amazing and incredible" because almost every student of Walt Whitman, and that includes those of us who love him as well, are convinced that it is simply not true. And, that the best explanation as to why Whitman invented this story, and placed it in the context of a letter about homosexuality, appears to be that he did not want to deal with questions about his own homosexual nature. His notebooks are full of references to this struggle – he often refers to them as "perturbations" – and they were a constant source of anxiety.

The questions of John Addington Symonds, Whitman's own concern about his "perturbations," his intimate relationships with young men like Peter Doyle, the obvious homoerotic nature of much of his poetry, raise some of the most interesting questions about Whitman, and about Leaves of Grass, about the "Calamus" poems. Reactions of students of Walt Whitman range from those who reject the notion of Whitman's homosexuality to those who see him as an active homosexual, with, it seems to me, the bulk of modern opinion being in the later camp. Whitman's response to a friend, late in his life, about the Symonds letters, may shed some light on those questions.

> Perhaps I don't know what it all means—perhaps never did know. Maybe I do not know all my meanings.

My own convictions about Whitman's sexuality falls some place between the two extremes. It seems to me that Walt Whitman was terribly confused about this own sexuality. All of his life he had to deal with questions, from within himself, about his own sexuality, questions which he never really resolved, except in his poetry. He could love women, but could never be sexually involved with them. And he could love men, but he could never be sexually involved with them, either, except in his poetry.

If it is true that the great prophet of love cannot express that love himself, on a physical level, then there is a very special poignancy to his sexual poems. I use that word "poignancy" with care because it has connotations of "touching," "appealing to the emotions," "moving," but also of pain. Here was a person who could not experience love on an intense, physical level, yet struggled -- continuously struggled—to get that kind of love into his poems. The image that comes to my mind, as I write these words, is Moses, the Moses who leads the people to the Promised Land but is never permitted to enter himself. Whitman should be loved, if only for that struggle.

E

"Calamus" is about the human need for intimacy. Whitman's response to the live oak, growing in a flat wide space without a friend or lover near, is a human response. Human beings as human beings need one another. We may have our individual identity, and at times need to assert it, but we also know that we feel incomplete and unfulfilled with out a close relationship, or close relationships. With Whitman, we know that we cannot be joyous without "a friend or lover near."

Whatever else such intimacy may be, it must at least be physical. It must be in the body. As human beings we need to literally touch, and be touched. There is something fundamentally human about Whitman's line in his poem about the doubts of appearances, and something incredibly sad about human beings who do not know it: "He ahold of my hand has completely satisfied me." Bodies need to be in loving contact with bodies.

From such a perspective it is not hard to understand that John Addington Symond's queries are answered by "Calamus" if not by Walt Whitman. If the self is, at root, the body; and if that body, and all parts of that body, are sacred; and if the body, and the functions of the body, and the needs of the body, are their own reason for being; and if physical intimacy is a sort of sacrament: then the pleasure two consenting adults feel in a caring relationship is sacred whether it is heterosexual or homosexual. The need to physically love and be loved, to find expression of our sexual beings, is universal, and the expression of that love is its own justification. That must be as true for homosexuals as it is for heterosexuals, even if the nineteenth century poet could not admit it.

We find satisfaction and fulfillment in sexual relationship, however, only in the context of caring, only as we both love and are loved. Lao Tzu has a line where he says that "Caring is an invincible shield against being dead." We find our aliveness in caring. We find our aliveness in reaching out to one another, with concern for both their own needs and ours. The idea is not using people to meet our needs, but sharing, in a caring relationship, with those we love.

Whitman's vision is ever expansive, moreover. It begins with the body and with the needs of the body, expands to include human intimacy on the most personal level, and continues to expand to embrace communities, nations, the world and, eventually, the human family across time. The ideal community is one where people really care about the needs of other people, where people really do care about what happens to other people, where people really do care about the legacies they are leaving for their children and grandchildren and all future generations.

Such a vision is, in the words of Whitman, "The base of all metaphysics." What he means by that is that such love is the foundation of any valid religion. The basis of valid religion is not found in dogmas or rituals or doctrines. It is found in the way actual human beings, with the natural gifts of these bodies, intimately, lovingly and with caring relate to one another, and relate to all others who share the same kind of bodies and the same kind of needs. This more than all else, Whitman might say, carries the hope of human salvation.

In his "Calamus" poem, "The Base of all Metaphysics," he recalls to mind all of the great philosophical and religious traditions of humanity – "The Greek and Germanic Systems;" "Kant," and "Fichte and Schelling and Hegel;" "Plato, and Socrates greater than Plato:" and "Christ divine" – and then places above all those great systems, his system:

> I see reminiscent to-day those Greek and Germanic systems,
> See the philosophies all, Christian churches and tenets see,
> Yet underneath Socrates clearly see, and underneath Christ the divine I see,
> The dear love of man for his comrade, the attraction of friend to friend,
> Of the well-married husband and wife, of children and parents,
> Of city for city and land for land.

CHAPTER VI
FOR LIFE, MERE LIFE

Thanks in old age – thanks ere I go,
For health, the midday sun, the impalpable air
  -- for life, mere life,
For precious ever-lingering memories,
        "Sands at Seventy"

A

In 1874 Walt Whitman wrote a very interesting poem called "Prayer of Columbus," which is presumably about the sufferings of Columbus on his last voyage and in his last years. When he published "Prayer of Columbus," Whitman prefaced the poem with an historical note:

> It was near the close of his indomitable and pious life—on his last voyage, when nearly seventy years of age—that Columbus, to save his two remaining ships from foundering in the Caribbean Sea in a terrible storm, had to run them ashore on the Island of Jamaica—where, laid up for a long and miserable year—1503—he was taken very sick, had several relapses, his men revolted, and death seemed daily imminent; though he was eventually rescued, and sent home to Spain to die, unrecognized, neglected and in want.....

Whitman begins his poem,

> A batter'd wreck'd old man
> Thrown on this savage shore, far, far from home,
> Pent by the sea and dark rebellious brows, twelve dreary months,
> Sore, stiff with many toils, sicken'd and nigh to death,
> I take my way along the island's edge,
> Venting a heavy heart.

The "I" in the poem is Columbus who says that his life is "full of woe," and who hopes that he might not live another day. As the "prayer" progresses, Columbus gives a report on his life and of his righteousness, much like Job in the Old Testament,

> All my emprises have been fill'd with Thee,
> My speculations, plans, begun and carried on in thoughts of Thee,
> Sailing the deep or journeying the land for Thee,
> Intentions, purports, aspirations mine, leaving results to Thee.

Columbus, thankful that God has lighted his life, continues his prayer,

> For that O God, be it my latest word, here on my knees,
> Old, poor, and paralyzed, I thank Thee.

Thinking the end is near, Columbus yields his ships to God, and then when all seems lost, "As if some miracle, some hand divine unsealed my lips," the miracle happens, the ships come to save him.

Whitman ends the "Prayer of Columbus" with these words,

> Shadowy vast shapes smile through the air and sky,
> And on the distant waves sail countless ships,
> And anthems in new tongues I hear saluting me.

On the surface this poem is about Columbus, but almost all students of Whitman see it as being essentially autobiographical. Walt Whitman had told his friend, Ellen O'Connor, about this poem, "I shouldn't wonder if I have unconsciously put a sort of autobiographical dash in it." More than a "dash," most students of Walt Whitman conclude, a full measure. The "battered and wreck'd old man" is Walt Whitman. The "old, poor and paralyzed" man is Walt Whitman.

B

In January of 1873, the year before he wrote "Prayer of Columbus," "twelve dreary months" before he wrote this poem, and after a long period of illness, Walt Whitman suffered a major stroke. The stroke left him, as he put it, "a half paralytic." The whole decade of the seventies was a very difficult time for Walt Whitman. The poet, who had once been proud of his body and of his health, saw his health fade and his body degenerate. The poet, who saw himself as becoming old before his time, felt a lot of despair. It was his world that was "full of woe," and it was he who hoped, that he might not "live another day."

Walt Whitman had spent a quarter of a century, by this time, trying to get a hearing for his Leaves of Grass, a lifetime really of seeking support for his vision of the western world. The lines in this poem that talk about such things as "all my emprises have been fill'd with Thee, My speculations, plans, begun and carried on in thoughts of Thee," are about his own commitment to his muse. Whitman clearly saw himself, as it is sometimes put, "explaining the ways of God to man." And now, in the wake of his stroke, it all seemed to be coming to naught. Whitman was profoundly discouraged. And yet he was also a man of faith. He was waiting for some miracle. He still had hopes that the message of his precious "Leaves" would still be heard. He still had hopes that he would hear "new tongues... saluting me."

Just about this time, however, just about the time of his stroke or about the time he wrote "Prayer of Columbus," Whitman became friends with another one of those young men who were always a part of his life. The name of this young man was Harry Stafford, and Harry introduced Walt to his parents, who were farmers in the New Jersey countryside. Whitman became close friends with all of the Staffords and spent considerable time at their farm. They even arranged a room for him in the farmhouse so that he could come and go and spend several days at a stretch. On the Stafford farm was a woods with a creek running through it, Timber Creek, and Timber Creek became the place where Whitman worked himself out of his depression and back to a place of better health. Whitman tells about his experiences on Timber Creek in his <u>Specimen</u> <u>Days</u>.

During the summers of 1876 and 1877, Whitman was at Timber Creek almost continuously. Every day the Stafford children would help the feeble old man walk down to the creek, one of them carrying a chair for him to sit in. The children were under instructions to leave him alone and he would stay there all day, by himself. Frequently he would take all of his clothes off, experience the fresh and warm air of summer, and let the curative powers of Nature work on his naked body. "As I walk'd slowly over the grass, the sun shone out enough to show the shadow moving with me," Whitman wrote in a segment titled "A Sun Bath – Nakedness," dated August 27, 1877.

> Somehow I seem'd to get identity with each and everything around me, in its condition. Nature was naked and I was also. It was too lazy, soothing, and joyous-equable to speculate about. Yet I might have thought somehow in this vein: Perhaps the inner never lost rapport we hold with earth, light, air, trees, &c., is not to be realized through eyes and mind only, but through the whole corporeal body, which I will not have blinded or bandaged any more than the eyes. Sweet, sane, still Nakedness in Nature! Ah if poor, sick, prurient humanity in cities might really know you once more. Is not nakedness then indecent? No, not inherently. It is your thought, your sophistication, your fear, your respectability, that is indecent. There come moods when these clothes of ours are not only too irksome to wear, but are themselves indecent.

Sometimes he would wrestle with the young saplings found along the creek side, swaying and yielding to their natural power. "I stand on the turf and take these health pulls moderately and at intervals for nearly an hour, inhaling great draughts of fresh air," he notes in a piece called "The Oaks and I," dated September 5, 1877,

> I can soon feel the sap and sinews rising through me, like mercury to heat. I hold on boughs of slender trees caressingly there in the sun and shade, wrestle with their innocent stalwartness—and know the virtue thereof of passes from them to me. (Or

may-be we interchange – may-be the trees are more aware of it all than I ever thought.)

As Walt Whitman basked in the summer's sun at Timber Creek, and wrestled with the young saplings, he came to feel "through his whole being," an "identity between himself subjectively and Nature objectively." Whitman feels a "presence at Timber Creek, as of Nature personified," which "neither chemistry nor reasoning nor esthetics will give the least explanation." "All the past two summers," he notes, [this presence] "has been strengthening and nourishing my sick body and soul, as never be-for."

> Thanks invisible physician, for thy silent delicious medicine, thy day and night, thy waters and thy airs, the banks, the grass, the trees, and e'en the weeds.

Slowly, ever so slowly, but surely, the "invisible physician," did its work and health began to return to the "half-paralytic." Walt Whitman never fully recovered, he remained somewhat impaired to the end of his days, but he was able to cope with the world. After the experience at Timber Creek he was no longer the "batter'd and wreck'd old man" of the "Prayer of Columbus." He was alive and the old love of life, which characterized his life's work, once again found expression in his very being.

A decade after those summers at Timber Creek, and two or three years before his death, Whitman wrote a little poem called "Thanks in Old Age." Perhaps in this poem, which is a celebration of life, there is a remembrance of those days at Timber Creek, and the new power which they brought to his body, and the lessons which they renewed for his mind.

Thanks in old age -- thanks ere I go,
For health, the midday sun, the impalpable air –
   for life, mere life,
For precious ever-lingering memories.

C

"Thanks," the poet says, "for life, mere life." Walt Whitman chooses his words carefully, so why the use of the word "mere?" The word is usually defined, as in The American Heritage Dictionary, as "being nothing more than what is specified," but it is also derived from the Middle English, "boundary." It seems to me that Whitman's meaning carries both connotations. At the deepest level, in his celebration of life, the poet is celebrating nothing more than this specific thing that has emerged out of nature with the particular boundary that defines "me." In his celebration of "mere life," Whitman is celebrating the very fundamental fact of existence.

"I too had received identity by my body," Whitman sings in "Crossing Brooklyn Ferry," and describes this identity as arising from the "eternal float of solution," which is the universe. The "float" is an ocean metaphor for the fluid nature of the matter of the universe that gives rise, at different times, to individual things and beings. Every individual, Whitman suggests, is "cohered together from its diffuse float." Whitman uses the same metaphor in "As I Ebb'd With the Ocean of Life,"

> I too have bubbled up, floated the measureless float,...
> I too but signify at the utmost a little wash'd up drift.

Whitman uses a different metaphor, in "Song of Myself," in his beautiful hymn of evolution, which concludes:

> All forces have been steadily employ'd to complete and delight me;
> Now on this spot I stand with my robust soul.

The "mere" fact of coming into existence, of having come out of the "substance" of the universe into this "self" and this particular "being," to live this particular "life," is cause for celebration. Apart from what life has to offer us, for good or ill, it is a wonderful thing to exist. "I am grateful for what I am and have," noted Henry David Thoreau, in words that express Whitman's intentions:

> My thanksgiving is perpetual. It is surprising how contented one can be with nothing definite – only a sense of existence. My breath is sweet to me...

We have come out of the "diffuse float" into this "self" and this "life," and have this wonderful capacity to know the world through our bodies! That is a wonderful thing. Whitman would have us become aware of what a wonderful thing it is to be. To be! -- with these bodies that can know and experience and love the world – with these eyes and ears and nerves which can quiver to the reality of life. G. K. Chesterton puts this thought in the past tense, in terms of having been,

> Lo, and blessed are our ears, for they have heard;
> Yea blessed are our eyes for they have seen;
> Let the thunder break on man and beast and bird,
> And lightning. It is something to have been.

Whitman puts his emphasis in the present sense, but means the same thing.

D

We can get an additional understanding of Whitman's "mere," in "mere life," if we think of it in terms of immortality. Walt Whitman believed in immortality, but never had a clear understanding of it, and always hedged his bets about the subject. In "On the Terrible Doubts of Appearances," he said he wonders if "identity beyond the grave is a beautiful fable only," and then concludes,

> I cannot answer the question of appearances or that
>   of identity beyond the grave,
> But walk or sit indifferent, I am satisfied,
> He ahold of my hand has completely satisfied me.

He is satisfied because, although he hopes for immortality, life itself is enough. It is enough to be. Whitman likes that world, "enough," and uses it repeatedly: "I exist as I am, that is enough," "enough to merely be! Enough to breathe;" "To be surrounded by beautiful, breathing, laughing flesh is enough." What ever may be the truth about immortality, life is enough!

"It seems to me that every thing in the light and air ought to be happy," Whitman says in one of his most mysterious poems, "The Sleepers," "Whoever is not in his coffin and the dark grave let him know he has enough." This is a hard teaching, but I believe that Whitman means it. He means it, that is, if you do not push the idea to an absolute. He is talking about being, just being. There may be circumstances where people, such as those in unrelievable pain, may prefer death to life, but Whitman is not talking about those extraordinary situations. In a world where people suffer, where life is sometimes full of disappointments, where life is not all that we would like it to be, -- and Whitman had his share of all of these things – we need to constantly remind ourselves of the miracle of being alive. As Whitman puts it in "The Mystic Trumpeter,"

> Joy! Joy! In freedom, worship, love! Joy in the ecstasy of life!
> Enough to merely be! Enough to breathe!
> Joy! Joy! All over joy!

E

Life is a miracle and we should rejoice in it. That is a basic message of the gospel of Walt Whitman. It is a wonder to have existence; it is a wonder to be. But Whitman's view of the sacredness of life does not stop at existence, it moves on to experience. It does not stop at being; it moves on to doing. It does not stop at life, it moves on to living. "We may trick with the word life in its dozen senses until we are weary of tricking;" Robert Louis Stevenson notes in some indicative words,

> We may argue in terms of all the philosophies on earth, but one fact remains true throughout—that we do not love life, in the sense that we are greatly preoccupied about its conservation. We do not, properly speaking, love life at all, but living.

Walt Whitman loved living. It was the concreteness of life, the actual fact of living life, that was of importance to him, and is intrinsic to his understanding of life. In this, as in all other matters, it is not abstractions that interest him. It is the living reality. As a boy, Walt Whitman loved roaming the fields and the shores of Long Island: that for him was living. As a young man he loved the ferries and would sometimes persuade the ferry captains to let him pilot them for a little while: that for him was living. And he loved the great omnibuses that ran up and down Broadway, and could ride on them for hours on end, sometimes taking reins in hand: that for him was living. During the Civil War he shared his life with countless wounded soldiers, played games with them, and gave them small gifts: that for him was living. Throughout most of his life, until illness prevented it, he was especially fond of walking. He would walk all over the cities of his life, and through the countrysides as well: that for him was living. As an old man he was able to travel into the Midwest, as far west as Colorado, and into Canada, to experience that which he had only read about: that to him was living. To be with people, to play with children, to visit family and friends, to go to the opera, to visit museums, to sell copies of his "book:" that for him was living.

This love of life, and of living, is also found all through Leaves of Grass. Unlike some of the other themes that are central to Whitman's prophetic vision, there is no collection of poems specifically committed to the theme of life, but the whole of Leaves of Grass is imbued with it. In "Song of Myself" Whitman identifies himself as the "caresser of life." In the very first "inscription" of his final edition of Leave of Grass, he sings, as if it is his dominant theme, "Of life immense in passion, pulse and power." In his "Song of Joys," Whitman lists the joys of life: "O the gleesome saunter over fields and hillsides!" "O to confront with your personality all the other personalities of the earth!" "O while I live to be the ruler of life, not a slave, to meet life as a powerful conqueror." He not only lists the things that are usually associated with joy, but also pain and hardship and suffering and sorrow and death. These are all part of the life which he celebrates.

His message is clear: in the midst of the totality of life, he would have us celebrate the ecstasy, the wonder, the glory of being:

> To dance, clap hands, exult, shout, skip, leap, roll on, float on!
> To be a sailor of the world bound for all ports!

Whitman's vision of the joyful life is not just a vision for the beautiful people, or for the young, or for the healthy. It is a vision for all people; a vision for people of all ages. "Youth, lusty loving – youth full of grace, force, fascination," Whitman asks in "Youth, Day, Old Age and Night," written near the end of his life, "Do you know that old age may come after you with equal grace, force and fascination?" The wonder of life, with its "grace, force, fascination," transcends age and finds expression wherever we might be in the cycle of existence. Perhaps it is most prevalent as we grow older and know how precious and dear, and short, life can be.

F

Is life worth living, is life something to celebrate, even in the midst of tragedy, despair, and grief? Walt Whitman's answer to this question is central to his prophetic vision. If we cannot celebrate life, there is nothing at all to celebrate. The meaning of life is to be found in living, if it is to be found at all. Whitman's prophetic vision as I have already suggested, begins with the self, the "self" that results from a merger of the soul and the body. Whitman's prophetic vision continues with a merger between the self that is the body and the very concreteness of life. Whitman himself had experienced tragedy and despair in his life and yet knew that here, in life, with these bodies, is the meaning of it all. D. H. Lawrence eloquently captures this essential quality of Walt Whitman's Prophetic vision:

> It is a great new doctrine. A doctrine of life. A new great morality. A morality of actual living, not of salvation. Europe has never got beyond the morality of salvation, America to this day is deathly sick with saviorism. But Whitman, the greatest and the first and the only American teacher, was no savior. His morality was no morality of salvation. His was a morality of the soul living her life, not saving herself.

The great new doctrine of Walt Whitman is "the soul living her life" – many souls living many lives. For Walt Whitman it is not the great people, or the great moments, or the great events, which are central to his prophetic vision. It is the common moments, and the common lives, of the mass of people, living ordinary lives, which is central. No doubt Walt Whitman would have said "amen" to Carl Sandburg's extension of his prophetic vision in a little poem with the simple title, "Happiness."

> I asked professors who teach the meaning of life to tell me what is happiness.
> And I went to famous executives who boss the work of thousands of men.
> They all shook their heads and gave me a smile as though I was trying to fool with them.
> And then one Sunday afternoon I wandered out along the Des Plaines River.

And I saw a crowd of Hungarians under the trees with their women and children and a keg of beer and an accordion.

CHAPTER VII
NOTHING ELSE BUT MIRACLES

> To me every hour of the light and the dark is a miracle,
> Every cubic inch of space is a miracle,
> Every square yard of the surface of the earth is spread with the same.
> "Miracles"

A

One of the great theological debates of the 19th century, at least among the Unitarians and other liberal Christians, centered on the question of miracles. The miracles in question were the miracles of Christ as reported in the New Testament, i.e., Jesus turning water into wine at the marriage in Cana, the raising of Lazarus form the dead, or walking on water. The controversy arose, when it did, because of the emergence of the scientific age. From the perspective of science, as it probed the mysteries of the world, the miracles seemed unscientific, unsupported by the evidence. The Biblical miracles did not appear sensible to the rational mind.

The traditionalists in this controversy maintained that the miracles, as reported in the New Testament, were literally true, and that one had to believe in the miracles as a central aspect of Christian faith. The radicals in this controversy, although thinking of themselves as Christians, primarily looked to nature – and Nature was usually spelled with a capital "N" – for inspiration, and saw the miracles as being in violation of the laws of Nature.

Most of the radicals in this controversy were transcendentalists. The transcendentalists believed that God was immanent in Nature—existing within, or inherent in, Nature—and that one knew the divine, intuitively, through a direct encounter with Nature. The revelation of the sacred, that is, came to the individual human being through his or her approach to world itself. "The Transcendentalist thesis," relative to the question of miracles, Perry Miller says in <u>The Transcendentalists</u>, was that

> Christianity is valid, not because it is recorded in history and attested to by miracles, but because it coincides with the intuitive nature of the mind.

Christianity is not proven by miracles, or by any other external form. Christianity is true, if it is true, because it impresses the mind with its truth.

The key figure in this controversy was Ralph Waldo Emerson. Emerson had been ordained as a Unitarian minister, but had given up the ministry and spent the rest of his life writing essays and giving public lectures. The transcendentalist character of Emerson's thought can be seen in a passage from one of the most important of his essays, "Nature."

> Why should not we enjoy an original relation to the universe? Why should not we have a poetry and philosophy of insight and not of tradition, and a

religion of revelation to us, and not the history of theirs? The sun shines also today. There are new lands, new men, new thoughts. Let us demand our own works and law and worship.

The central event in the controversy over miracles was an address given by Emerson to the graduating class of Harvard Divinity School in 1838. In that address, which is usually referred to as the "Divinity School Address," Emerson called upon the graduating students, soon to become active ministers, to become "new born bards of the Holy Spirit," and to seek the revelation of the sacred, not through books or religious tradition, but by direct encounter of the mind with the world. "One is constrained to respect the perfection of this world in which our senses converse," Emerson told the Harvard seniors, and then, in words that apply directly to our theme, added:

> [Christ spoke of miracles] for He felt that man's life was a miracle, and all that man doth, and he knew that his daily miracle shines, as the character ascends. But the word miracle, as pronounced by Christian churches, gives a false impression; it is a monster. It is not one with the blowing clover and the falling rain.

Thoughts like these provoked an immediate response which was very hostile. The leader in this hostile response was Andrews Norton, a Unitarian professor of theology at Harvard, who called Emerson's ideas, "The latest form of infidelity."

> The latest form of infidelity is distinguished by assuming the Christian name, while it strikes directly at the root of faith in Christianity, and

indirectly of all religion, by denying the divine miracles attesting the divine mission of Christ.

Conservative Unitarians felt that belief in the miracles was necessary for Christianity to endure. Richard Hildreth, a young Unitarian minister and a transcendentalist, summarized Andrews Norton's views, and other orthodox Christian views, in this way:

> The only ground then, in your opinion, which we can possibly have for placing any confidence in one who claims to be a messenger from God, is the fact that he works miracles. The fact of his working miracles is the only evidence we can have of his divine mission, and of the truth of what he undertakes to reveal.

The transcendentalists on the other hand, with their view of direct experience, and with their reverence for Nature, felt no need to dwell on the miracles as recorded in the New Testament. There were so many miracles to be observed in Nature, they felt, that there was nothing so particularly miraculous about Biblical miracles. George Ripley, an eloquent defender of transcendentalism, although he himself affirmed belief in the Biblical miracles, felt that the modern age required a reexamination of the miracles.

> We live in an age of skepticism and vague thought on many of the most important subjects of belief; but for myself I am certain that no cold reserve, no coward's fear, no spiritual despotism can remove or mitigate the evil. We want scientific inquiry and discussion, in which the love of truth shall be blended with a heartfelt trust in its power. I see most clearly the work that is to be done for this age,

before a return to deep religious conviction is possible.

B

One of those who saw most clearly "the work that is to be done for this age," was Walt Whitman. Although Walt Whitman was never a transcendentalist, in the sense that he embraced it as a particular doctrine, some of the ideas it expressed formed an essential part of his own belief system. Whitman was indebted to Ralph Waldo Emerson – "I was simmering, simmering, until Emerson brought me to a boil" – and is often seen as responding to Emerson's call for a new class of poets. Whatever may have been the sources of his inspiration, however, Whitman's <u>Leaves of Grass</u> is permeated with the idea that "the distinction between the divine and the natural ceases to mean anything at all when Nature is seen as a divine language."

"I will thread a thread through my poems that time and events are compact," Whitman says in "Starting From Paumanok," "and that all things of the universe are perfect miracles, each as profound as any." Walt Whitman sees miracles everywhere he looks, and sees in those miracles profound religious truths that books or priests could never reveal: "A morning glory at my window satisfies me more than the metaphysics of books." Miracles are not Supernatural events, they are commonplace events.

Elizabeth Barrett Browning says the same thing in her "Aurora Leigh:"

> Earth's crammed with heaven
> And every common bush aflame with God:
> But only he who sees takes off his shoes,

The rest sit around it and pluck blackberries.

For Walt Whitman, clearly, earth is literally "crammed with heaven." Whitman is constantly taking off his shoes. The poet knew full well what that other Moses discovered before that other burning bush: "The place whereon thou standeth is holy ground." All places and things are for him "holy ground." No other poet sees that "holy ground" in the common things of earth with such exquisite, delicate, and eloquent words, as does Walt Whitman. In his very first major poem, "Song of Myself," he articulates – in the form of a credo – the common miracles of Nature:

> I believe a leaf of grass is no less than the journey-work of the stars,
> And the pismire is equally perfect and a grain of sand, and the egg of a wren,
> And the tree-toad is a chef-d'oeuvre for the highest,
> And the running blackberry would adorn the parlors of heaven,
> And the narrowest hinge in my hand puts to scorn all machinery,
> And the cow crunching with depress'd head surpasses any statue,
> And a mouse is miracle enough to stagger sextillions of infidels.

I have always loved that last line: "A mouse is miracle enough to stagger sextillions of infidels." It is almost as if, with his use of the word "infidel," Whitman were speaking directly to Andrews North who protested "the latest form of infidelity." The true infidelity, according to Whitman's gospel, is to fail to see the divine in nature. The true fidelity is to recognize that divinity every time you turn around. Do you see that miracle in that grain of sand? How is "walking on water" superior to that as a miracle? Do you see the miracle in that "cow crunching with depress'ed head?" How is turning water into wine superior to that as a miracle? Do you see that miracle in that "egg of a wren?" How is the virgin birth superior to that as a miracle? And the hinge in your hand? Think about it. What a remarkable thing this hand is, with its many tiny bones and muscles, and opposable thumb! The things it can do! How can any of the miracles of the Bible compare to the miracle of the human hand!

"Miracles need not be sought in special occurrences, in phenomena which startle us out of our ordinary way of regarding the universe," John Addington Symonds says in his study of Walt Whitman:

> Whitman expels miracles from the region of mysticism only to find a deeper mysticism in the world of which he forms a part, and miracles in commonplace occurrences. He dethrones the gods of the old pantheons, because he sees God everywhere around him.

C

"I believe a leaf of grass," Whitman says, "is no less than the journey-work of the stars." In those words his concept of miracles expands from the smallest of things, the grass, to the grandest of things, the stars. These, and all that lie between them are, for Whitman, the realm of miracles. He often talks of grass – "the good green grass, that delicate miracle, the ever-recurring grass"– because grass is his ultimate symbol, the connecting thread of <u>Leaves of Grass</u>. In one of his earliest notebooks he wrote that it was his intention to confound the "learning of all times" with a single blade of grass. Grass is everywhere, all over the globe. Whitman called it the "uniform hieroglyphic," by which he means, I think, that grass is the key both to his poetry and to his prophetic vision.

Hieroglyphics was an ancient Egyptian form of writing which involved the use of pictures. For centuries, no one knew how to decipher those hieroglyphics, until a stone was discovered, the Rosetta Stone which had the same quotation engraved upon it in both hieroglyphics and in Greek. A Frenchman, Champollion, is credited with deciphering the Rosetta Stone and, in the process, making the hieroglyphics intelligible. I believe that the figures on the Rosetta Stone, which was discovered in 1799, and deciphered in 1821, and of Champollion, loom behind Whitman's symbol of the grass.

"This is the grass that grows wherever the land is and the water is," Whitman sings in "Song of Myself," "This is the common air that bathes the globe." Grass is the symbol of the most common, and if one can find the sacred, the miraculous, in the most common, then one can find it in all things in the universe. "Soon shall the winter's foil be here; soon shall these icy ligatures unbind and melt," Whitman sings in a lovely little poem anticipating the coming of spring,

> A little while,
> And air, soil, wave, suffused shall be in softness,
>   bloom and growth – a thousand forms shall rise
> From these dead clods and chills as from low burial
>   graves.
> Thine eyes, ears – all thy best attributes – all that
>   takes cognizance of natural beauty,
> Shall wake and fill. Thou shalt perceive the simple

shows, the delicate miracles of earth.
Grass, the most common, is one of the "delicate miracles" of earth. And, if that is so, then the other plants, and the animals that inhabit earth, must also be miracles. And, if that is so, then human beings must also be miracles. "Divine am I, inside and out," the poet says of himself, and of all selves, "Seeing, hearing, feeling, are miracles and each part and tag of me is a miracle." That is why he can say, without egotism, "If I worship one thing more than another it shall be the spread of my body, or any part of it."

For Whitman the vision continues to expand, the mountains and the seas and the clouds and the sky are all miracles. The earth itself is a miracle. And the sun and the stars. "The sun and stars that float in the open air," Whitman says in "A Song for Occupations,"

> The apple-shaped earth and we upon it, surely the
>   drift of them is something grand,
> I do not know what it is except that it is grand.

"All the things of the universe," Whitman insists, "are perfect miracles."

D

In one of his best known poems, "When I Heard the Learned Astronomer," Whitman talks about going to a lecture and listening to "the astronomer where he lectured with much applause in the lecture-room." The lecture was replete with figures, "ranged in columns before me," and with charts and diagrams. After a while the poet decided he had enough:

> How soon unaccountable I became tired and sick,

> Till rising and gliding out I wander'd off by myself,
> In the mystical moist night-air, and from time to time,
> Look'd up in perfect silence at the stars.

Sometimes, when people read this poem, they see it as a rejection of the astronomer, or as the rejection of science. Any one who knows Walt Whitman, however, would know that this is not the case. He loved astronomy and was reasonably well versed in the astronomy of his time. No doubt he was among those who applauded the astronomer as he lectured. But there comes a time when one must stop learning about something and experience it for one's self. Whitman left the lecture to go outside to experience the miracle of the stars.

At one point in his life Walt Whitman read an article, whose author is now anonymous, titled "Imagination and Fact." The poet underlined a sentence that particularly impressed him and wrote a note in the margin. The sentence that impressed Whitman was, "The mountains, rivers, forests, and the elements that gird them round about would be only blank conditions of matter if the mind did not fling its own divinity around them."

Whitman's marginal comment: "This I think is one of the most indicative sentences I have ever read." Things would be only things, if we did not "fling divinity around them." That was central to Walt Whitman's prophetic vision. It was his gospel to "fling divinity around" everything, to see the miraculous in all things. "That only which we have within can we see without," Emerson wrote, "If we see no gods, it is because we harbor none." Walt Whitman could see God, and miracles, in the whole unfolding wonder of creation.

E

"Why should I wish to see God better than this day?" Whitman asks in "Song of Myself," "I find letters from God dropt in the street ---and every one is sign'd by God's name." The letters from God are the miracles of everyday life. The letters from God are in the people, the things, the events, the moments of human existence. This theme is reiterated all through Leaves of Grass. This theme is intrinsic to an understanding of the prophetic vision of Walt Whitman:

> If you would understand me go to the heights or water-shore,
> The nearest gnat is an explanation, and a drop or motion of waves a key,
> The maul, the oar, the hand-saw, second my words.

Towards the end of his life Whitman gathered all of these thoughts together in a single little poem which he called "Miracles."

> Why, who makes much of a miracle?
> As to me I know of nothing else but miracles,
> Whether I walk the streets of Manhattan,
> Or dart my sight over the roofs of houses toward the sky,
> Or wade with naked feet along the beach just in the edge of the water,
> Or stand under trees in the woods,
> Or talk by day with any one I love, or sleep in the bed at night with anyone I love,
> Or sit at table at dinner with the rest,
> Or look at strangers opposite me riding in the car,
> Or watch honey-bees busy around the hive of a

summer forenoon,
Or animals feeding in the fields,
Or birds, or the wonderfulness of the sundown, or stars shining so quiet and bright,
Or the exquisite delicate thin curve of the new moon in spring;
These with the rest, one and all, are to me miracles,
The whole referring, yet each distinct and it its place.

To me every hour of the light and dark is a miracle,
Every cubic inch of space is a miracle,
Every square yard of the surface of the earth is spread with the same,
Every foot of the interior swarms with the same.

To me the sea is a continual miracle,
The fishes that swim – the rocks – the motion of the waves – the ships with men in them,
What stranger miracles are there?

CHAPTER VIII
THE CENTRE OF ALL DAYS

> I know that the past was great and the future will be great and I know that both curiously conjoint in the present time,
> And that where I am or you are this present day, there is the centre of all days, all races,
> "With Antecedents"

A

Walt Whitman was born on May 31, 1819, at West Hills on Long Island in New York. When young Walter was four years old his family moved to Brooklyn and he lived there through the remainder of his childhood and well into adulthood. Long Island was home to him, and as he says,

> The successive growth stages of my infancy, childhood, youth and manhood were all pass'd on Long Island, which I sometimes feel as if I had incorporated. I roam'd as boy and man, and have lived in nearly all parts, from Brooklyn to Montauk Point.

Whitman did "incorporate" Long Island into his very being and this is reflected throughout his poems. The images he saw there, the experiences he had there, with the ocean, with the farmer's fields, with the birds and the people, left an indelible mark upon him that was never to be forgotten or ignored. Whitman presented some exquisite descriptions of the place in his <u>Specimen Days</u>.

There is an Indian name for Long Island which Whitman preferred, and always used as a code word for his origins. The Indian name for Long Island is Paumanok and it is described in <u>Specimen Days</u> in words attributed to John Burroughs, but seems very much to me as if they were, in fact, words Burroughs got from Whitman.

> Paumamok...over a hundred miles long; shaped like a fish--plenty of sea shore, sandy, stormy, uninviting, the horizon boundless, the air too strong for invalids, the bays a wonderful resort for aquatic birds, the south-side meadows cover'd with salt hay, the soil of the island generally tough, but good for the locust-tree, the apple orchard, and the blackberry, and with numberless springs of the sweetest water in the world.

Paumanok was a special place for Walt Whitman and his poetry, a symbol for his own beginnings and origins and a symbol for beginnings and origins in general. The first major collection of poems in the final edition of <u>Leaves of Grass</u>, which define the entire theme of the book, is called "Starting from Paumanok."

B

"Starting From Paumonak" is placed early in <u>Leaves of Grass</u>, because it deals with the poet's origins and with his ideas about origins in general. Once again the reader must be aware of the poetic use of the word "I" in Whitman. He is talking about Walt Whitman, about his origins, but sees this as but a concrete expression of the origins of human beings. Other "I"s have different origins but they all came out of a place, their own particular place.

"Starting from fish-shaped Paumanok where I was born," Whitman begins the first untitled poem in this section and ends it with "Solitary, singing in the west, I strike up for a New World." He then goes on to one of his catalogues, one of his lists, naming some of the experiences between the then and the now: "Well begotten, and rais'd by a perfect mother;" "Roaming many lands, lover of populous pavements;" "Dweller in Manhattan my city" "or in a soldier's camp;" "having studied the mocking-bird," the "mountain hawk," "and heard at dawn the unrival'd one, the hermit thrush." What Whitman is doing here, in the content of this poem, is presenting an outline of his life. That life began in Paumanok, as a baby, but as he grew he gathered unto himself many experiences, many scenes, and these are, in his present, part of his being and part of his way of looking at the world.

This theme is picked up in one of his most beautiful and powerful pieces, "There Was a Child Went Forth," which was included in the first edition of <u>Leaves of Grass</u>, but which was revised in later editions and placed in the "Autumn Rivulets" section. It begins,

> There was a child went forth every day,
> And the first object he look'd upon, that object he became,
> And that object became part of him for the day or a certain part of the day,
> Or for many years or stretching cycles of years.

Whitman then goes on to "name," in beautiful imagery, in an exquisite word picture, sights and moments and experiences in his childhood, examples of the things he had become, and had become part of him. There are natural things like "the early lilacs" and "the sow's pink-faint litter," and of a boy looking into the waters of a pond and seeing the "fish suspending themselves so curiously below there, and the beautiful curious liquid." There are images of people like the "tidy and fresh cheeked girls" and the "friendly" or "quarrelsome boys" in the schoolyard, or, in a more humorous vein, of "the old drunkard staggering home from the outhouse of the tavern whence he had lately risen."

His parents are here, too, "he that had fathered him and she that had conceived him in her womb and birthed him," who gave him "more of themselves," and "became a part of him." Here is the mother with her "mild words, clean cap and gown, a wholesome odor falling off her person." And the father, "Strong, self-sufficient, manly, mean, anger'd, unjust." Here also is a memory of a traumatic event in the household: "the blow, the quick loud word, the tight bargain, the crafty lure." In the midst of all this an "affection that will not be gainsay'd" and a "sense of what is real."

Here, too, are his cities, Brooklyn and New York, with "The streets themselves and the facades of houses, and goods in the windows," and "the schooner near by," in the bay, "sleepily dropping down the tide." And there is the ocean, always the ocean, with its "hurrying tumbling waves." With these and many other images in mind, Whitman concludes the poem:

> These became part of that child who went forth every day, and who now goes, and will go forth every day.

C

Think of a lens, which the American Heritage Dictionary defines as a "carefully molded piece of glass, by means of which light rays are refracted so they converge or diverge to form an image." There are three lenses through which the above accounts from "Starting from Paumonak" and "There was a Child Went Forth" are "refracted" to form an image. There is the lens of the self, the lens of place, and the lens of time. The lens of the self is Walt Whitman. The lens of place is Paumonak. The lens of time is the middle of the 19th century.

Again, think of the word, "focus," which refers to "a point to which something converges or diverges" in order to present a "sharply or clearly defined" image. Three things come into "focus" in these accounts of experiences from Whitman's life – the self, place, and time – all of which are expressed in the most concrete form possible. If one is to understand Walt Whitman and his message, if one is to gain an understanding of his prophetic vision, one needs to understand this important point. The meaning "of life immense," Whitman's religion, is always "refracted" through the lens of concrete experience, always comes into focus in the self, in place, and in time.

I have chosen the word "focus", at this point, with careful deliberateness. It is derived from a Latin word which means "fireplace, hearth, the center of the home." The religious values of Walt Whitman find their expression in the things that are "closest to home."

The first "focal point" is the concrete self. "One world is aware and by far the largest to me, and that is myself," Whitman says in "To You," "I am he who places over you no master, owner, better, God, beyond what intrinsically waits in yourself." "You are asking me questions and I hear you," Whitman adds in "Song of Myself,"

> I answer that I cannot answer, you must find out for yourself.
>
> You must habit yourself to the dazzle of the light and of every moment of your life.

"You must find out for yourself." The meaning of life is always refracted through individual experience. That thought is central to Walt Whitman's prophetic vision, as he clearly states in "Song of Myself."

> You shall no longer take things at second or third hand, nor look through the eyes of the dead, nor feed on specters in books,
> You shall not look through my eyes either, nor take things from me,
> You shall listen to all sides and filter them from your self.

In <u>Leaves of Grass</u> the real emphasis is always on "you." You must use your senses to absorb the world around you. You must appropriate the knowledge that is available to you. You must create for yourself your own understanding of the religious verities. Here is how Whitman puts it in his "Song of Occupations:"

> We consider Bibles and religions divine – I do not say they are not divine,
> I say they have all grown out of you, and may grow out of you still,
> It is not they who give the life, it is you who give the life.

"Leaves are not more shed from the trees, or trees from the earth, than they are shed out of you," Whitman says, in a play on words. The "leaves" are, of course, his own <u>Leaves of Grass</u>, which were "shed" out of himself. Your "leaves" must be "shed" from yourself. You must develop for yourself your own vision of what is true and good and beautiful. Even my "leaves," Whitman is saying, should not be your guide, which is why he always insists, as he does in "Song of Myself," "He most honors my style who learns under it to destroy the master."

"I call that mind free which jealously guards its intellectual rights and powers, which does not content itself with a passive or hereditary faith," William Elery Channing, perhaps the most significant preacher of the first half of the 19th century, writes, "Which opens itself to light whencesoever it may come; which receives new truth as an angel from heaven." Channing's words can underscore the heart of the Whitman message. His prophetic vision does not call for allegiance to a hereditary faith. And it is certainly not "passive." "Who are you that wanted only to be told what you knew before? Who are you that wanted only a book to join you in your nonsense?" Whitman fairly shouts in "By Blue Ontario's shores,"

> Piety and conformity to them that like,
> Peace, obesity, allegiance, to them that like,
> I am he who tauntingly compels men, women, nations,
> Crying, Leap form your seats and contend for your lives!

"Leap from your seats and contend for your lives!" That spirit pervades all of <u>Leaves of Grass</u>. That is the mandate Whitman sets before what he calls "the true poets." They are challenged to struggle with the world and to force it to mean. It is the same challenge that he sets before every human being. We must contend with our world, struggle with our world, and force it to mean, force it to reveal to us, and in ourselves, the meaning of our days.

Whitman's religion is not one of salvation, it is one of seeking. One can see that Whitman was profoundly influenced by his family's Quaker background, even if he himself did not belong to that faith. As a little boy, Walt Whitman went to hear the great liberal Quaker preacher, Elias Hicks, and a love of Hicks stayed with him all of his life. In his collected prose there is an article that Whitman wrote about this man whom he, Whitman, considered a prophet.

> Elias taught throughout, as George Fox began it, or rather reiterated and verified it, the Platonic doctrine that the ideas of character, of justice, or religious action, whenever the highest is at stake, are to be conform'd to no outside doctrine or creeds, Bibles, legislative enactments, conventionalities, or even decorums, but are to follow the inward Deity-planted law of the emotional soul.

For Whitman, as for the Quakers, the inner light, and not the outward authorities, is to guide people in matters of religious faith. I do not know if Walt Whitman would have known these words from Gautama, the founder of Buddhism, but I expect that he would have loved them:

> Be ye lamps unto yourselves;
> Be your own confidence.
> Hold to the truth within yourself,
> As to the only lamp.

One can also see in the gospel of Walt Whitman, the influence of the transcendentalists, in general, and of Ralph Waldo Emerson, in particular. "I can find Greece, Asia, Italy, Spain, and the islands – the genius and creative principle of each and all eras – in my own mind," Emerson wrote in his essay on "History,"

> Every mind must know the whole lesson for itself.
> What it does not see, what it does not live, it will
>   not know.

> I am the owner of the sphere,
> Of the seven stars and the solar year,
> Of Caesar's hand, and Plato's brain,
> Of Lord Christ's heart, and Shakespeare's strain.

In terms of Walt Whitman's gospel, the individual must "own" his own experience, must create and write his own gospel.

D

The first of the three lenses I have mentioned is the lens of the self. In the prophetic vision of Walt Whitman, the meaning of life is "refracted" through the individual self; through one's own concrete being. The other two lenses involve time and place. The meaning of life is "refracted" through one's own time and one's own space location. This is how Whitman states the premise in "With Antecedents."

> I know that the past was great and the future will be great,
> And I know that both curiously conjoint in the present time,
> ...
>
> And that where I am or you are this present day, there is the centre of all days, all races,
> And there is the meaning to us of all that has ever come of races and days, or ever will come.

"Where I am or you are this present day," Whitman insists, "there is the center of all days." It is not that Whitman rejects the past or the future – "I know that the past was great and the future will be great" – but that both the past and the future come into focus in and through the present. The past and the future, to use Whitman's interesting words, "curiously conjoint" in the present. The word "conjoin" is a verb which means to "join together, to connect, unite." The word "conjoint," an adjective, refers to "joined together, connected, united." There is an active quality to the present in Whitman's prophetic vision. The past finds its fruition in the present, and the future finds its possibilities there. In that context we can find our meaning only in the present, only in that active context. We can live neither in the past or in the future, we can only live in the present. As Whitman puts it,

Will you seek afar off? You surely come back at last,
In things best known to you finding the best, or as good as the best...
Happiness, knowledge, not in another place but this place, not for another hour but this hour.

"Finding the best, or as good as the best," Whitman writes, "not in another place but this place, not for another hour but this hour." This may not be the best of all possible worlds, but it is our best world. We will not have any other world to live in. If we are going to find "happiness, knowledge," we are going to find it in this world, in our place, in our time. "This time, like all other times, is a very good one," Emerson said, "if we but know what to do with it." Whitman knew what to do with it. In the gospel according to Walt Whitman, we are called upon to embrace it, to love it, to rejoice in it. This is our chance to be! In our present, at this place and time, in the living of our lives, for Whitman, eternity comes into focus.

"Who, constructing the house of himself or herself, not for a day but for all time," Whitman says in "Kosmos" in his collection called "Autumn Rivulet," "sees races, eras, dates, generations, the past, the future, dwelling there, like space, inseparable together." The "who" in these words, the "Kosmos," is that person who recognizes that the universe comes into focus, at this time, in his or her own being. Whitman's preference for the Greek spelling, "Kosmos," Gay Wilson Allen explains, "which came from the Sanskrit cad, 'to distinguish one's self,' indicates emphasis on independent order and harmony as an attribute of his own divinity." In the sacredness of the human individual, in the sacredness of the concrete moment and the concrete place, eternity finds expression. Walt Whitman would have

embraced the thoughts of Richard Jeffries, as expressed in
<u>The Story of My Heart</u>.

> It is eternity now. I am in the midst of it. It is all about me, in the sunshine: I am in it, as the butterfly in the light-laden air. Nothing has to come; it is now. Now is eternity; now is the immortal life.

For Whitman the sacred finds being in the present. We need to accept it, love it, and find the meaning of our lives in it. Anne Gilchrist, Whitman's "greatest woman friend," in "An Englishwoman's Estimate of Walt Whitman," captures the idea with power,

> Out of the scorn of the present came skepticism; and out of the large loving acceptance of it comes faith. If now is so great and beautiful, I need no arguments to make me believe that the nows of the past and of the future were and will be great and beautiful too.

E

In the great religions of the western world – Judaism, Islam, and Christianity – the focal point is located somewhere in the past. In Judaism, that focal point is the Exodus, the time when Moses led the children of Israel out of Egypt. In Islam, the focal point is the Heigira, the flight of Mohammed form Mecca to Medina. The Islamic Calendar dates time from that event, beginning, according to the standard western calendar, July 16, 622 AD. The Christian year begins with the birth of Christ. All time is measured in terms of the Christ event, before Christ and after Christ.

Christian theologians sometimes think of the Christ event as "the hinge of history." Using the same analogy, the hinge of history for Jews would be the Exodus, and the hinge of history for Islam would be the Hiegira. A "hinge" is defined as "a jointed or flexible device permitting turning or pivoting...." or "a point on which subsequent events depend." The great religions of the western world hinge, or to use Whitman's word, "conjoint" at some point in the past. They turn or pivot on specific events in the past. The meaning of the present is intrinsically linked to some point in the past on which all "subsequent events depend."

The gospel of Walt Whitman rejects all of this. The prophetic vision of Walt Whitman finds the "hinge of history" in the present. The hinge of history is located in the most concrete person, in the most concrete location, at the most concrete moment in time."

"I was looking for a long while for Intentions, for a clew to the history of the past for myself, and for these chants—and now I have found it," Whitman sings in "Autumn Rivulets,"

> It is not in those paged fables in the libraries, (them
>   I neither accept or reject,)
> It is no more in the legends than in all else,
> It is in the present --- it is in this earth to-day,
> It is in the life of one man or one woman to-day....

This aspect of the prophetic vision of Walt Whitman is also found in the ancient Sanskrit, in words attributed to Kalidasa.

Look to this day!
For it is life, the very life of life.
In its brief course lie all the verities and realities of
    your existence:
The bliss of growth,
The glory of action,
The splendor of beauty,
For yesterday is but a dream,
And tomorrow is only a vision:
But today, well lived, makes every yesterday a
    dream of happiness
And every tomorrow a vision of hope,
Look well, therefore, to this day.

CHAPTER IX
WHERE THE GREAT CITY STANDS

> A great city is that which has the greatest men and women,
> If it be a few ragged huts it is still the greatest city in the whole world.
> "Song of the Broad-Axe"

A

Most people will recognize Walt Whitman as a significant poet, many will remember his heroic work in military hospitals during the Civil War, some may recall that he was, for a number of years, a newspaper editor, but few people, I expect, have ever thought of Walt Whitman as a political figure. Politics was, however, an important part of his life.

In the years just before and just after the publication of the first edition of Leaves of Grass, Whitman was the editor of numerous newspapers: on Long Island, the Long Islander; in New York City, the Aurora; in Brooklyn, the Daily Eagle; and in New Orleans, the Crescent. All in all, Whitman worked for ten or more newspapers in the major media centers of the new world.

The newspapers of that period were particularly political, moreover, and as an editor, Whitman was deeply involved in the political issues of his time as a writer, as a speaker, and as an organizer.

Some knowledge of this political background is necessary for understanding the social aspects of Whitman's prophetic vision, and of his honorific title as "Poet of Democracy." Walt Whitman became involved in the political life of New York while he was still in his teens. His involvement was with the Democratic Party and, at that early age, he was mostly involved as a campaigner. By the time he was twenty-one, however, his position in the party was such that he was asked to speak at a Democratic rally, in New York, at which eight to ten thousand people were present. That speech, in which he proclaimed, "It is our creed – our doctrine not a man or set of men, that we seek to build up," is an early example of his democratic idealism. His speech was published in The Evening Post.

By the time he was in his middle twenties he had been elected secretary of the Brooklyn Democratic organization and was a member of Tammany Hall in New York. That was when Tammany Hall was still an important and idealistic Democratic institution, committed to political reforms in favor of the common man, and not yet corrupted by political bosses such as William M. Tweed. Throughout that decade Whitman edited several Democratic newspapers all committed to the principles of the Democratic Party.

By the end of the decade of the 1840's, Whitman had become a leader among the Free-Soil Democrats – or "Barnburners" as they were often called – who opposed the extension of slavery into the territories and in the emerging western states. The Barnburners were northern Democrats who insisted on keeping slavery out of the new states even if this meant alienating Democrats in the south. This controversy led to a split in the Democratic Party and a convention was held in Buffalo to establish a new party on free-soil principles. Whitman was a delegate from New York to that convention and was one of the speakers there. He lost his job as editor of the <u>Brooklyn Daily Eagle</u>, which he referred to as "the best sit of my life," because he refused to compromise on the "free-soil" issue.

Political and social issues were always part of Whitman's prophetic agenda. Frequent attempts in modern times to make him out as a socialist miss the mark, however, because Whitman was all of his life a democrat: at times a Democrat with a capital "D" and other times with a lower case "d," but always within the historic value system of the Democratic Party. He was committed to the capitalist system, although he was well aware of its defects and its problems. And he felt that through this system the political rights of the common people could best be preserved. All of this is an aside, in some sense, however, because it is all prelude to his life as a poet, and his work as "The Poet of Democracy,"

> I speak the pass-word primeval, I give the sign of democracy, By God! I will accept nothing which all cannot Have their counterpart of on the same terms.

B

Walt Whitman is, as many have noted, "The Poet of Democracy." Henry David Thoreau may have been the first to recognize this when he said, of Whitman: "He is apparently the greatest democrat the world has ever seen." Whitman is also the prophet of democracy. His vision of democracy and of the democratic republic is central to his prophetic vision. "Perhaps he is the most ardent democrat living," noted O.B. Frothingham, a noted Unitarian minister in 1883, "He is severe because he hopes so much and sees so much at stake in the experiment of liberty." Frothingham was right. Whitman was a most ardent democrat and his severity and hope, which are central to his vision, find most complete expression not in his poetry, but in his remarkable prose work called <u>Democratic Vistas.</u>

Perhaps to adequately understand Whitman's vision of, and for, democracy, we have to look for the meaning of the word "democracy" on three different levels. Whitman moved back and forth between these three levels, but understood that in their connectedness and totality, they form the substance of a democratic republic and of a democratic world. It is not too much to say, furthermore, that Whitman's view of democracy is the central tenet in his religion. "For I say at the core of democracy, finally, is the religious element," Whitman says in <u>Democratic Vistas</u>, and adds elsewhere in the same work:

> I say that democracy can never prove itself beyond cavil, until it founds and luxuriantly grows its own forms of art, poems, schools, theology, displacing all that exists, or that has been produced anywhere in the past, under opposite influences.

In the first instance Walt Whitman views democracy as a political system. By that is meant that he saw democracy, as opposed to monarchy or totalitarianism, as involving, in a concrete and political sense, the sovereignty of the people. He believed in the town meetings. He believed in the ballot box. He believed in elections and the responsibility of elected officials to serve the electorate. Nothing was as invigorating for him as a good political campaign in which the people got involved with the politicians on matters of important public issue. At the center of this process is the citizen, who is both sovereign and the recipient of democratic activity. This is an article of political faith with him, as he says in "Song of Occupations."

> The president is there in the White House for you, it is not you who are here for him,
> The Secretaries act in their bureaus for you, not you for them,
> The Congress convenes every Twelfth-month for you,
> Law, courts, the forming of States, the charters of cities, the going and coming of commerce and mails, are all for you.

In this political definition of democracy he saw the citizen as central to the process. There is the requirement in any valid political democracy that people get involved. He stated his conviction in the first person in "Song of Myself," but, as is usually the case with his poetry, it is expected that the "I" will become the reader:

> This is the city and I am one of the citizens,
> Whatever interests the rest interests me, politics, wars, markets, newspapers, schools
> The mayor and councils, banks, tariffs, steamships, factories, stocks, stores, real estate and personal estate.

A second element in Whitman's view of democracy involves democracy as an organizing principle. He looked out at the world, and back through time, and saw the organizing principles—monarchies, feudalism, slave societies, etc. – and found all of them wanting. They do not fit the needs of the modern world. Whitman looks at democracy as it finds expression in America, and finds it wanting as well:

> I say that our New World, however great a success in uplifting the masses...is, so far, an almost complete failure in its social aspects and in really grand religious, moral, literacy and esthetic results.

But in spite of his frustrations and disappointments at what has happened to democracy in his beloved America, a frustration and a disappointment that often borders on despair, Whitman always arrives at the point, in the end, where he reaffirms it as the proper course for the modern world.

The third element in Whitman's definition of democracy involves seeing democracy as a belief system, or as a religious system. For Walt Whitman "Democracy," which he always spells with a capital "D," is written into the very nature of things, into the very nature of the universe. It is not only an organizing principle, it is <u>the</u> organizing principle. It is the only political system which recognizes the inherent authenticity and dignity of the human individual. It is the only organizing principle that resonates with the universe in recognition of the "self" that is at the heart of all things, that is the universe aware of itself.

Some people have referred to this aspect of Whitman's view of democracy as a "spiritual democracy," and one can see why in the following passage from <u>Democratic Vistas</u>.

> There is, in sanest hours a consciousness, a thought that rises, independent, lifted out from all else,

calm, like the stars, shining eternal. This is the thought of identity—yours for you, whoever you are, as mine for me. Miracle of miracles, beyond statement, most spiritual and vaguest of earth's dreams, yet hardest basic fact, and only entrance to all facts. In such devout hours, in the midst of the significant wonders of heaven and earth (significant only because of the Me in the center), creeds, conventions, fall away and become of no account before this simple idea. Under the luminousness of real vision, it alone takes possession, takes value. Like the shadowy dwarf in the fable, once liberated and look'd upon, it expands over the whole earth, and spreads to the roof of heaven.

C

"Democracy!" Walt Whitman exults in "Stating from Paumanok," "Near at hand to you a throat is now inflating itself and joyfully singing." It is hard to overestimate the importance of passages such as this when one is considering the prophetic vision of Walt Whitman. It lies at the very heart of his message. Democracy, as he understands it, is at the core of his religious vision for the new world and for a new age.

At the very heart of Whitman's theory of democracy is the idea of equality. His celebration of the "single, separate self" finds a social and political dimension in the doctrine of equality. The individual has ultimate value and is, therefore, of ultimate value in any authentic social or political system.

Whitman's celebration of equality is the celebration of the common human being. It is set in contradistinction to older systems of social organization: the citizen is seen as in no way subservient to a master, as a subject is to a king. In Whitman's view of the true democracy, the lowest of the citizenry is equal to mayors and governors and even presidents. One of Whitman's curious terms for this idea is that of "the divine average." "O such themes –equalities! O divine average!" Whitman sings in "Starting from Paumanok,"

> Strains musical flowing through ages, now reaching hither,
> I take to your reckless and composite chords, add to them, and cheerfully pass them forward.

When Whitman speaks of the "divine average," he is speaking of the common folk; or, better perhaps, of the uncommon potentiality of the common folk. A true democracy has to be built on a foundation of common people – not on one of politicians, or bankers, or merchants or industrialists – but on workers and farmers and housewives, and clerks. "Everything comes out of the people, the people as you find them and the people as you leave them," Whitman told his friend Horace Traubel, "People, people, just people."

The poet would have certainly endorsed Lincoln's phrase, "government of the people, by the people, for the people," but one can get a greater feel for Whitman's perspective, perhaps, if one adds the modifier "common" to each of those phrases: "government of the common people, by the common people, for the common people."

Government exists for the common people. The sole authentic and legitimate function of government, in terms of Whitman's vision of democracy, is to enable the human being – in the factory, in the home, on the farm – to totally and completely develop his or her potential. It is from this perspective that Whitman opposes slavery and supports women's suffrage. The slave cannot fulfill his or her potential while in bondage and the woman cannot fulfill her potential while she is relegated to the status of a second-class citizen. That government which permits slavery and which denies full citizenship to women is, therefore, an unauthentic and illegitimate government.

"The true office of government is simply to preserve the rights of each citizen from spoilation," Whitman wrote in one of his early editorials, "When it attempts to go beyond this, it is intrusive and does more harm than good." Whitman seems to have believed this all of his life. But he also believed that the "common" citizen had his or her responsibilities to fulfill as well. A democracy is only as great as the greatness of the people in it. A democracy cannot be great if its citizens only look out for themselves and their own welfare. The "common people" must develop the inherent and "latent" potentiality within themselves to be supportive of the "common good." Whitman underscores this thought in a powerful passage from Democratic Vistas:

> That which really balances and conserves the social and political world is not so much legislation, police, treaties, and dread of punishment, as the latent eternal intuitional sense in humanity, of fairness, manliness, decorum etc. Indeed this perennial regulation, control, and oversight, by self-suppliance, is sine qua non to democracy; and a highest, widest aim of democratic literature may well be to bring forth, cultivate, brace and strengthen this sense, in individuals and society.

In the context of Whitman's vision of Democracy, the "divine average" finds expression in the "divine aggregate." When common human beings discover their own "greatness" they can then create a great society. Whitman is always interested in the individual, but he is not only interested in the individual, he is also interested in the social structures which aware, caring, and committed human beings can create. One of the words Whitman uses to describe this is the French word, "en masse," which literally means "body," and which is defined in the American Heritage Dictionary as "in one group or body; all together." The individual "body" and the collective "body" are of equal importance to the poet. Democracy "seeks not only to individualize but to universalize," Whitman writes in Democratic Vistas:

> The great word Solidarity has arisen. Of all the dangers to a nation...there can be no greater one than having certain portions of the people set off from the rest by a line drawn.... To work in...and justify God, his divine aggregate, the People...this, I say, is what democracy is for; and this is what our America means, and is doing.

This concept of democracy is of such importance to Whitman that the very first lines of Leaves of Grass contain this affirmation:

> One's-self I sing, a simple separate person,
> Yet utter the word Democratic, the word En-Masse.

D

Walt Whitman's vision of Democracy is both idealistic and metaphysical. Democracy – and America, which is for

Whitman the symbol of democracy – are not realities, but potentialities. They are also, from Whitman's perspective, inevitable potentialities. More than that, they "will be:" they will find historic expression in the world. Democracy is the inevitable outcome of the workings of nature and of history. Democracy is, for Whitman, a law of the universe. Democracy as divine law finds expression in Whitman's poem titled "Thou Mother With Thy Equal Brood." The "Mother" in the poem is America and the "Equal Brood" is the American citizenry. "Belief I sing, and preparation;" Whitman wrote,

> As Life and Nature are not great with reference to
>   the present only,
> But greater still from what is yet to come,
> Out of that formula for thee I sing.

The "formula," his vision of democracy, is for the future, "from what is yet to come." "Sail, sail thy best, ship of Democracy," he goes on, "Of value is thy freight, 'tis not the present only." Of greatest value to the poet is the idea of democracy, the "freight," an idea which will find fruition in some future. The past is also there; it is in the past where the first glimpses of Democracy are to be found. The completion is to be found in the future. Walt Whitman sees his role as a poet/prophet of Democracy, as he sees the role of all "true poets," as one who proclaims the true nature of Democracy and seeks to bring it into existence. "I watch thee advancing, absorbing the present, transcending the past," he says of America as a potential expression of Democracy,

> I see thy light lighting, and thy shadow shadowing,
>   as if the entire globe,

> But I do not undertake to define thee, hardly to
>   comprehend thee,
> I but thee name, thee prophesy, as now,
> I merely thee ejaculate!

What the poet cannot entirely "comprehend" or "define" is, however, as I have said, inevitable. It will be comprehended and it will be defined in reality because it is "set in the sky of law:"

> (Lo, where arise three peerless stars,
> To be thy natal stars my country, Ensemble,
>   Evolution, Freedom,
> Set in the sky of Law.)

The destiny of America, of Democracy, is preordained. It had its "natal" beginnings, its birth, in the American Revolution but through the processes of historic evolution it will find its completeness through the whole world, a world which will be characterized by "freedom." I find Whitman's word "ensemble" to be very interesting and perhaps, even, insightful. There are a variety of definitions for that word. The first one given in the <u>American Heritage Dictionary</u> reads: "A unit or group of complementary parts that contribute to a single effect."

A primary example of "ensemble" is "a group of musicians, singers, dancers, or a troupe of players who perform together." I expect that Whitman had all of these thoughts in mind as he inserted the word "Ensemble," which he capitalized, in this poem. He always loved music and he always loved the theater, and I expect that he admired the way people could work together to produce a moving effect. Democracy was like the symphony or like the theater. People working together in harmony and in unison could produce a good world and a good society. That may not be happening in the present, but the process has begun and will find its conclusion. The last words of "Thou Mother with Thy Equal Brood" are these:

> Thou globe of globes! Thou wonder nebulous!
> By many a throe of heat and cold convuls'd, (by these thyself solidifying,)
> Thou mental, moral orb – thou New, indeed new, Spiritual World!
> The Present holds thee not – for such vast growth as thine,
> For such unparallel'd flight as thine, such brood as thine,
> The future only holds thee and can hold thee.

Although it has its roots in the past and is growing in the present, only the future holds the key to the shape of the true Democracy. When one looks at the present, however, with its injustice, its greed, its inequality, one despairs. Whitman sometimes despaired. There is no better example of this, I suppose, than his polemic called "The Eighteenth Presidency," in which he laments the fact that not "one in a thousand" public leaders are concerned with the common good, or in <u>Democratic Vistas</u>, in which he concludes:

> Never was there, perhaps, more hollowness at heart than at the present, and here in the United States. Genuine belief seems to have left us.... We live in an atmosphere of hypocrisy throughout...A scornful superciliousness rules in literature...Conversation is a mass of badinage. From deceit in the spirit, the mother of all false deeds, the off spring is already incalculable... The official services of America, national, state and municipal, in all their branches

and departments, except the judiciary, are saturated in corruption, bribery, falsehood, maladministration, and the judiciary is tainted.... It is as if we were somehow being endowed with a vast and more thoroughly appointed body, and then left with little or no soul.

But he also voices his despair in his poetry, such as in "I Sit and Look Out," where his melancholy and his sadness is articulated in a particularly poignant way:

> I sit and look out upon all the sorrows of the world, and upon all oppression and shame,
> I hear secret convulsive sobs from young men at anguish with themselves, remorseful after deeds done,
> I see in low life the mother misused by her children, dying, neglected, gaunt, desperate,
> I see the wife misused by her husband, I see the treacherous seducer of young women,
> I mark the ranklings of jealousy and unrequited love attempted to be hid, I see these sights on the earth,
> I see the workings of battle, pestilence, tyranny, I see martyrs and prisoners,
> I perceive a famine at sea, I observe the sailors casting lots who shall be kill'd to preserve the lives of the rest,
>
> I observe the slights and degradations cast by arrogant persons upon laborers, the poor, and upon negroes, and the like;
> All these --- all the meanness and agony without end I sitting look out upon,
> See, hear and am silent.

There are times when Whitman looks out at injustice, inequality and greed of the world and is silent. He is sometimes overcome, as we are all sometimes overcome, with the distance between the real and the ideal. Walt Whitman knows despair and he knows pessimism.

But Whitman's pessimism is always only momentary. In the end his optimism wins out; his ideal vision transcends the reality of the present world. The passage from Leaves of Grass which best exemplifies Whitman's ability to transcend his disillusionment is found in "The Song of the Broad-Ax." In the poem the poet describes the character of the "Great City," which provides a fulfillment of his prophetic vision:

> What do you think endures?
> Do you think a great city endures?
> Or a teeming manufacturing state? or a prepared
>   constitution? or the best built steamships?
> Or hotels of granite and iron? or any chef-d'oeuvres
>   of engineering, forts, armaments?
>
> Away! These are not to be cherish'd for themselves,
> They fill their hour, the dancers dance, the
>   musicians play for them,
> The show passes, all does well enough of course,
> All does very well till one flash of defiance.
> A great city is that which has the greatest men and
>   women.
> If it be a few ragged huts it is still the greatest city
>   in the whole world.
>
> The place where a great city stands is not the place
>   of strech'd wharves,
> docks, manufacturers, deposits of produce merely,

Nor the place of ceaseless salutes of new-comers, or
    the anchor-lifters of the departing,
Nor the place of the tallest and costliest buildings or
    shops selling goods from the rest of the earth,
Nor the place of the best libraries and schools, nor
    the place where money is plentiest,
Nor the place of the most numerous population.

Where the city stands with the brawniest breed of
    orators and bards,
Where the city stands that is belov'd by these, and
    loves them in return and understands them,
Where no monuments exist to heroes but in the
    common words and deeds,
Where thrift is in its place, and prudence is in its
    place,
Where the men and women think lightly of the
    laws,
Where the slave ceases, and the master of slaves
    ceases,
Where the populace rise at once against the never-
    ending audacity of elected persons,
Where fierce men and women pour forth as the sea
    to the whistle of death pours its sweeping and
    unript waves,
Where outside authority enters always after the
    precedence of inside authority,
Where the citizen is always the head and ideal, and
    President, Mayor, Governor and what not, are
    agents for pay,

Where children are taught to be laws to themselves,
    and to depend on themselves,
Where equanimity is illustrated in affairs,
Where speculations on the soul are encouraged,

Where women walk in public processions in the
    streets the same as the men,
Where the city of the faithfulest friends stands,
Where the city of the cleanliness of the sexes
    stands,
Where the city of the healthiest fathers stands,
Where the city of the best-bodied mothers stands,
There the great city stands.

E

The vision of the Great City lies at the heart of Walt Whitman's enduring theory of democracy and is central to his prophetic vision. That vision embraces liberty, equality, and justice, but like everything else in his religious scheme, is predicated on the notion of the sacredness, on the infinite worth of the human individual.

But Whitman's vision is not one of the solitary individual. It is one of individuals working together to build a better society, a better nation, and a better world. The sacred individual, along with other individuals – the "divine average" and the "divine aggregate" – bound together by the love which the poet expresses as "adhesiveness" – work together to create the "Great City." This is, for Walt Whitman, "The Base of All Metaphysics."

And now gentlemen,
A word I give to remain in your memories and
    minds.
As base and finale too for all metaphysics.
(So to the students the old professor,
At the close of his crowded course.)
Having studied the new and antique, the Greek and
    Germanic systems,

Kant having studied and stated, Fichte and Schelling and Hegel,
Stated the lore of Plato, and Socrates greater than Plato,
And greater than Socrates sought and stated, Christ divine having studied long,
I see reminiscent to-day those Greek and Germanic systems,
See the philosophies all, Christian churches and tenets see,
Yet underneath Socrates clearly see, and underneath Christ the divine I see,
The dear love of man for his comrade, the attraction of friend to friend,
Of the well-married husband and wife, of children and parents,
Of city for city and land for land.

CHAPTER X
JOURNEYERS WITH THEIR WOMANHOOD

I am the poet of the woman as well as the man,
And I say it is as great to be a woman as to be a man,
And I say there is nothing greater than the mother of men.
                    "Song of Myself"

A

In 1952 <u>The Saturday Review</u> published an essay by the noted anthropologist Ashley Montagu with the curious title "The Natural Superiority of Women." "Women have been conditioned to believe that they are inferior to men, and they have assumed that what everyone believes is a matter of fact," Montagu says in that essay, but the "evidence proves the superiority of woman to man." He does not use the word "superiority" to suggest "higher nature or character," he writes, but in "its common sense of being of better quality." For "evidence," Montagu points to the sex chromosomes, to the fact that male offspring comes only from the Y chromosomes, and then concludes that

> ...the sad fact is that the Y-chromosome is but an iota, the merest bit of a remnant of an X-chromosome; it is a crippled X-chromosome. The X-chromosomes are fully developed structures; the Y-chromosome is the merest comma. It is as if in the evolution of sex a particle one day broke away from an X-chromosome, and thereafter in relation to X-chromosomes could produce only an incomplete female-the creature we now call male! It is to this original chromosomal deficiency that all the various troubles to which the male falls heir can be traced.

This "chromosomal deficiency" prevents the male from having babies, and puts the male at a disadvantage as to competence in "social understanding" which the capacity for having children provides. Men have more trouble loving and are more aggressive, while women are more loving and more cooperative. "...it is precisely in this capacity to love and unaggressiveness that the superiority of women to men is demonstrated," he writes,

> For whether it be natural to be loving and cooperative or not, so far as the human species is concerned, its evolutionary destiny, its very survival is more closely tied to this capacity for love and cooperation than with any other. So that unless men learn from women how to be more loving and cooperative they will go on making the kind of mess of the world which they have so effectively achieved thus far.

"There can no longer be any doubt of the constitutional superiority of the female," Montagu goes on, "physically and psychically women are by far the superiors of men." Especially is this the case in the modern world, Montagu concludes, where "It is the function of women to teach men how to be human."

What the world stands so much in need of at the present time, and what it will continue to need if it is to endure and increase in happiness, is more of the maternal spirit and less of the masculine. ...The best of all ways in which men can help themselves is to help women realize themselves. This way both sexes will come for the first time fully into their own, and the world of mankind may then look forward to a happier history than it has thus far enjoyed.

"Women superior to men? This is a new idea," Montagu says in his essay, "There have been people who have cogently, but apparently not convincingly, argued that women were as good as men, but I do not recall anyone who has publicly provided the evidence or even argued that women were better than or superior to men." Apparently Montagu had not heard of Eliza W. Farnham. In 1864, almost a century before "The Natural Superiority of Woman," Eliza W. Farnham published a pioneering book in women's rights titled Woman and Her Era. Her conclusion:

> Woman is biologically the most advanced and virtuous form thus evolved by nature and that she is destined to become intellectually and spiritually superior to man as soon as she has divested herself of the prohibitions forced upon her by a male-dominated society.

This sounds very much like the thesis of Montagu's essay. Although Eliza Farnham is unaware of twentieth century knowledge about genes and chromosomes, she touches on many of the same themes and arrives at many of the same conclusions, as does Ashley Montagu. <u>Woman and Her Era</u> is a nineteenth century forerunner of "The Natural Superiority of Women."

Eliza Farnham published her book in 1864, nine years after Walt Whitman introduced his <u>Leaves of Grass</u> to the world. In this book she recognizes Whitman as a feminist, and proclaims him to be the only genuine "poet of woman." To underscore her feelings for Whitman, Eliza Farnham uses some lines from "Song of the Broad-Axe," in which Whitman expresses his idealistic view of woman, as an epigraph for her book:

> She is the best belov'd, it is without exception, she has no reason to fear, and she does not fear...
> She is silent, she is possess'd of herself, they do not offend her,
> She receives them as the laws of Nature receive them, she is strong,
> She too is a law of Nature – there is no stronger law than she is.

Walt Whitman may not have been the only poet in the history of the world to envision an era "in which woman shall have triumphed," but there are few other male literary figures in the nineteenth century who place so much stress on the equality of women, on the rights of women, and on the need for women to be accepted into full citizenship. When Whitman sings his prophetic anthem, found in "By Blue Ontario's Shores" – "I am for those who walk abreast with the whole earth, Who inaugurate one to inaugurate all" – the "all" includes in an absolute, and emphatic sense, women. The radical themes suggested by Eliza Farnham's book and by Ashley Montagu's essay are largely shared by Walt Whitman. The most powerful expression of this shared theme is found in a poem called "Unfolded Out of the Folds," which is located in a collection called "Autumn Rivulets."

> Unfolded out of the folds of the woman man comes unfolded, and is always to come unfolded,
> Unfolded only out of the super best woman of the earth is to come the super best man of the earth,
> Unfolded out of the friendliest woman is to come the friendliest man,
> Unfolded only out of the perfect body of a woman can a man be form'd of perfect body,
> ….
> Unfolded out of the strong and arrogant woman I love, only thence can appear the strong and arrogant man I love,
> Unfolded by brawny embraces from the well-muscled woman I love, only thence comes the brawny embraces of the man,
> Unfolded out of the folds of the woman's brain come all the folds of the man's brain, duly obedient,
> Unfolded out of the justice of the woman all justice is unfolded,
> Unfolded out of the sympathy of the woman is all sympathy;
> A man is a great thing upon the earth and through eternity, but every jot of the greatness of man is unfolded out of woman;
> First the man is shaped in the woman, he can then be shaped in himself.

B

Walt Whitman as a person and Walt Whitman as a poet was "unfolded" out of many women. He would be the first to credit his mother, Louisa Van Velsor, with a Dutch strain predominating in her temperament, as the major influence in his life and the source of his poetic inspiration. But there were many other women from the literary world, "strong and arrogant," who helped to shape both Whitman's personality and his prophetic vision. Three who were especially important to Whitman, and whose impact can be seen in both Leaves of Grass and his prose writings, were Frances Wright, George Sand, and Margaret Fuller. All three of these women were feminists, "strong and arrogant," and helped to shape Walt Whitman's prophetic vision.

The first of these important women was Frances "Fanny" Wright, a Scottish-born freethinker, feminist, and reformer who spent a number of years in America before returning to her home in Europe in 1839. Whitman's father, who had a radical mind of his own, took Walt, as a boy, to hear Frances Wright talk about the "Religion of Humanity," the idea that a religion for the modern world must incorporate the best aspects of all cultures, and about the needs for reforms in the way American society treated women, slaves, and the laboring class. In 1829, when Walt Whitman was yet a young man, she became one of the editors of The Free Inquirer to which the Whitmans subscribed. The young Walt Whitman read the new magazine carefully and it helped to shape his thoughts. The family had a copy of Wright's book A Few Days In Athens, which touted her epicurean philosophy – "the first and last thing I would say to man is, think for yourself" – a book which Whitman cherished all his life and which became threadbare with use.

Walt Whitman referred to Frances Wright as "Glorious Frances," and when the Whitman family went to hear her speak, he said, "Her very presence seemed to enthrall us." Wright profoundly influenced Whitman's life. Her themes of human equality, of social justice, and of liberating religion found echoes in all of his future work. In his later years Whitman made a great tribute to this great woman who he said was, for many years, his "daily bread," and whom he considered "one of the best in history." Whitman said of Frances Wright that she was

> One of the few characters to excite in me a wholesale respect and love: she was beautiful in bodily shape and gifts of soul.... I never felt so glowingly towards any other woman.... She possessed herself of my body and soul.

A second "strong and arrogant woman" that profoundly influenced Walt Whitman was the French novelist, George Sand whose given name was Amantine Lucile Aurore Dupin. George Sand, who was always a champion of progress and reform, was a committed socialist who opposed every form of slavery, championed the rights of women and the working class, and promoted the cause of human solidarity. Margaret Fuller, who visited her in France, saw in George Sand "a goodness, nobleness and power that pervades the whole."

Just as the works of Frances Wright were found in the Whitman home, so were the novels of George Sand, and the young Walt Whitman read them eagerly. He always enjoyed the philosophical character of these novels and was moved by Sand's idealism. Two of his favorite novels by George Sand were <u>Consuelo</u> and its sequel <u>Countess of Rudolstadt</u>. Whitman said of his copy of <u>Consuelo</u>, which had belonged to his mother and which he had read as a boy, that he read it so often that the sheets [were] often loose and ready to drop out. He was so fond of the book that he told his friends that he thought Consuelo superior as a character to any of Shakespeare's heroines.

It is the Countess of Rudolstadt, however, that is most interesting in thinking about Walt Whitman. Esther Shephard has written a book, Walt Whitman's Pose, in which she sees the source of Whitman's work in the epilogue of this book. The epilogue describes a poet prophet who is a Christlike figure, dressed in carpenter's clothes, who falls into a trance and proceeds to write a great and perfect poem. Whitman seems to have adopted this "pose" as his own. Esther Shephard felt that this was the source of both his great and lovely poetry and the lists and platitudes which are sometimes found in Leaves of Grass.

While it may be far too much to expect that the epilogue of The Countess of Rudolstadt provided the source of Leaves of Grass, it is no doubt true that the novels of George Sand had an important affect on the emerging poet. From her he received the persona he was to build upon for the rest of his life, and from her he got many of the notions of strong and liberated women whom he would have populate his new world. He also received from George Sand a commitment to social reform and political equality. And from her he received some aspects of his view of religion.

George Sand, who had spent some of her early years in a convent school, was a deeply religious person who, nevertheless, always distrusted organized religion, especially members of the clergy. Part of her reason for this was that she felt religion was involved in the process of keeping women in bondage and of keeping women in an inferior position in human society. "Deliberately, women are given a deplorable education," she wrote in one of her Letters to Marcie, 1837, "While man frees himself from constraining civil and religious bonds, he is only too glad to have woman hold tightly to the Christian principle of suffering and keeping her silence." As he went about the task of articulating his own religious vision, Walt Whitman always insisted that adequate religion should be a liberating force and not an enslaving one, and that women should be a central facet of the whole religious enterprise.

The third "strong and arrogant woman" from which the "strong and arrogant man" was to be unfolded was Margaret Fuller. Although they had never met, Whitman was quite familiar with her work, and admired her greatly.

For several years Margaret Fuller was a reporter and columnist for Horace Greeley's New York Tribune, and at one point published a number of her pieces in a book titled Papers on Literature and Art. Whitman reviewed this book in the Brooklyn Eagle, while he was editor, and kept a copy to the end of his life. "Books which imitate or present the thoughts of and life of Europe do not constitute an American literature," Margaret Fuller wrote, "Before such can exist, an original idea must animate this nation and fresh currents of life must call into life fresh thoughts along its shores." This is precisely what Walt Whitman tried to do in Leaves of Grass. He committed his life to an attempt to create a literature which was not beholden to the old world, but represented, in bold strokes, a new world.

Margaret Fuller's most important contribution to literature, however, was Woman in the Nineteenth Century, 1845, which was the first major feminist treatise in America, a treatise which did for America what Mary Wollstonecraft had done for England a half century earlier in her great work, <u>Vindication of the Rights of Women</u>. Fuller's book, which became an instant sensation in Europe as well as America, provided nourishment for the emerging women's rights movements all around the world. "Ye cannot believe it, men," she was to write, "but the only reason why women ever assume what is more appropriate to you is because you prevent them from finding out what is fit for themselves."

Margaret Fuller, along with husband and her baby, were killed in a shipwreck in 1850, off the coast of Long Island, which Walt Whitman called by its Indian name, Paumanok. Walt Whitman and Margaret Fuller had never met, but he thought of her often as he walked the shore line that he loved so well and he undoubtedly incorporated her into his vision of the strong, liberated, self-sufficient woman. He had come to agree with her when she wrote,

> I would have woman lay aside all thought, such as she habitually cherishes, of being taught by men. I would have her free from compromise, from complaisance, from helplessness, because I would have her good enough and strong enough to love one and all beings, from the fullness, not the poverty of being.

C

Walt Whitman shared Margaret Fuller's vision of a new world where women are permitted to live "from the fullness, not the poverty of being." His vision of a world where women are equal with men, a world where women's right are an established reality, finds expression throughout <u>Leaves of Grass</u>, but, perhaps, it finds its most complete expression in his prose works. In <u>Democratic Vistas</u>, and also in <u>An American Primer</u>, Whitman attempts to articulate a new vision for America, a new vision for democracy, a new vision which will underwrite what he refers to as a "new dispensation," or a "new sociology," of a fully developed and authentic democratic republic. One important and prominent aspect of this vision is the establishment of the rights of women. He writes:

> I have sometimes thought that the sole avenue and means of a reconstructed sociology depends primarily on a new birth, elevation, expansion, invigoration of woman, affording for ages to come (as the conditions that antedate birth are indispensable), a perfect motherhood. Great, great, indeed far greater than they know, is the sphere of women.

Basic to this "reconstructed sociology," he goes on, is achieving

> the entire redemption of women out of these incredible holds and webs of silliness, millinery, and every kid of dyspeptic depletion – and thus insuring to the States a strong and sweet female race, a race of perfect mothers.

Whitman believed that what he was envisioning, furthermore, will come to pass:

> The day is coming when the deep question of woman's entrance amid the arenas of practical life, politics, the suffrage, etc., will not only be argued all around us, but may be put to decision and real experiment.

Contemporary feminists, who read these words for the first time, will be struck by the constant reference to women as mothers. Whitman does exalt motherhood, and sees in mothers the hope of the future, the hope of giving birth to, and raising children who will establish a new democratic order. But his exaltation of motherhood is also a characteristic of the feminism of the time. "We must educate our daughters to think that motherhood is grand," his great contemporary Elizabeth Cady Stanton declared:

> If you suffer, it is not because you are cursed by God, but because you violate his laws. What an incubus it would take from woman could she be educated to know that the pains of maternity are no curse upon her kind.... But one word of fact is worth a volume of philosophy; let me give you some of my own experience. I am the mother of seven children. My girlhood was spent mostly in the open air. I early imbibed the idea that a girl is just as good as a boy and I carried it out.

Both Walt Whitman and Elizabeth Cady Stanton, as was common in those days, defined women in terms of motherhood, but underneath this perspective is a more profound conviction: the conviction that women, as women, are equal with men and should have all the rights and privileges that pertain to men in any just society. Throughout his writings Whitman seems to echo the thoughts of his great liberal contemporary on the other side of the ocean, John Stuart Mill, such as the paragraph from Mill which is, or at least was, on the stationary of NOW, the National Organization of Women.

> The principle which regulates the existing social relations between the sexes – the legal

subordination of one sex to the other – is wrong in itself, and one of the chief hindrance to human improvement. It ought to be replaced by a principle of perfect equality, admitting no power or privilege on the one side, nor disability on the other.

One extremely interesting aspect of Whitman's thought on this matter has to do with the question of language. Whitman always used expressions like "him or her" or "he and she" rather than the generic "he" or "him," and always tended to emphasize the female as well as the male. The poet saw almost a century and a half ago the need to revise the language so that equality between the sexes would be expressed in everyday language. Whitman, who had a great reverence for the power of words, saw that words can be a vehicle of oppression and that new words are needed to deal with both the new realities and the democratic potentiality. He expresses this thought in <u>An American Primer</u>:

> In America an immense number of new words are needed to embody the new political facts...words to answer the modern, rapidly spreading, faith of the vital equality of women with men and that they are to be placed on an equal plane, socially and in business with men.

D

The attitude toward women which Walt Whitman expressed in his prose works, and the expressions of women's rights and human equality which are found there, also find expression in the poetry of <u>Leaves of Grass</u>. In his very first poem, "Song of Myself," Whitman sets forth his feminist agenda:

> I am the poet of the woman as well as the man,
>
> And I say it is as great to be a woman as to be a man,
> And I say there is nothing greater than the mother of men.

In his "Song of Occupations" he expands upon the theme, suggesting the equality of women in all of her many roles: i.e. as a wife, as a mother, as a daughter.

> The wife, and she is not one jot less than the husband,
> The daughter and she is just as good as the son,
> The mother, and she is every bit as much as the father.

In the "Children of Adam" poems, with their more explicit sexual content, Whitman affirms the rights of women as sexual beings. Just as Whitman's mature man "knows and avows the deliciousness of his sex," the mature woman "knows and avows the deliciousness of hers." For Whitman the human body is sacred because "it is the soul," as was noted in the early chapters of this book. The human body, Whitman says, "balks account," by which he means that we do not have to explain it, we just have to accept it. It is a part of our natural and sacred being. And this is as true for women as it is for men.

> The love of the body of man or woman balks account, the body itself balks account,
> That of the male is perfect, and that of the female is perfect.

Whitman has the same kind of attitude towards feminine

sexuality and sexual passion. For Whitman it is sexual passion which makes life worthwhile and it must therefore find full and complete expression in human life. To be totally human one must accept and embrace one's own sexuality.

This thought carries over into Whitman's concept of motherhood. The modern woman, who would become the mothers of a great race of human beings, Whitman felt, must be free and joyous in her own sexuality. Woman, as mothers, have a very special place in Whitman's theory, as was noted above, perhaps, even a superior place. In a world where women were expected to be ashamed of their sexuality, Whitman desired that they embrace it with the superior awareness that they are not only "the gates of the body," but also, "the gates of the soul." Women, that is, are not only the physical mothers of human life, but also that which brings creativity into the world. The poet elaborates on this in "I Sing the Body Electric."

> Be not ashamed women, your privilege encloses the
>   rest, and is the exit of the rest,
> You are the gates of the body, and you are the gates
>   of the soul.

It is particularly interesting to note the positioning of Eve in the last poem of "Children of Adam." The two generic human beings, the male and the female, are leaving the garden, that is, leaving the past world where the man was the "lord and master," and entering a new world of human liberation and equality. No longer did Eve have to follow Adam. She could lead, or she could follow, or she could just walk by his side.

> Existing I peer and penetrate still,

> Content with the present, content with the past,
> By my side or back of me Eve following,
> Or in front, and I following her just the same.

The strong, liberated woman which Whitman feels will populate the new world is sketched in vivid images in "A Woman Waits for Me."

> They are not one jot less than I am,
> They are tanned in the face by shining suns and blowing winds,
> Their flesh has the old divine suppleness and strength,
> They know how to swim, row, ride, wrestle, shoot, run, strike, retreat, advance, resist, defend themselves,
> They are ultimate in their own right – they are calm, clear, well possess'd of themselves.

E

Walt Whitman says of his poem "A Woman Waits For Me" that it is a poem illustrative of the women under "the new dispensation," "...the best mothers—the healthiest women – the most lovely women." In that poem Whitman says of women that they are "ultimate in their own right." This thought is central to an understanding of the prophetic vision of Walt Whitman. Whitman supported total women's rights for the very same reason he opposed slavery and favored abolition: the new world and the new dispensation could only be composed of people who were free to develop, in the most complete form, their own potentialities. Without that ability the world was crippled and could not become what it was capable of becoming. In his preface to the 1872 edition of <u>Leaves of Grass,</u>

Whitman defined America as "not the man's nation only, but the woman's nation – a land of splendid mothers, daughters, sisters, wives." This was just four years after Susan B. Anthony began publication of her women's suffrage newspaper <u>The Revolution</u>, with its motto "Men their rights and nothing more; women their rights and nothing less." Although the great poet had never met the great feminist, they shared a vision of America, and of the world; a world in which great womanhood as well as great manhood was necessary. The strong and liberated individual, female and male, with their vast potential for the creation of goodness, provide an important aspect of the core of Whitman's prophetic vision. He celebrates this in a poem titled "To You," which is found in "Birds of Passage".

> Whoever you are, now I place my hand upon you,
>   that you be my poem,
> I whisper with my lips close to your ear,
> I have loved many women and men, but I love none
>   better that you.
>
> O I have been dilatory and dumb,
> I should have made my way straight to you long
>   ago,
> I should have blabb'd nothing but you, I should
>   have chanted nothing but you.
>
> I will leave all and come and make the hymns of
>   you,
> None has understood you, but I understand you,
> None has done justice to you, you have not done
>   justice to yourself,
>
> None but has found you imperfect, I only find no

imperfection in you,

None but would subordinate you, I only am he who will never consent to subordinate you,
I only am he who places over you no master, owner better, God, beyond what waits intrinsically in yourself.

CHAPTER XI
NO MORE SAD, UNNATURAL SHOWS OF WAR

> Away with themes of war! Away with war itself!
> Hence from my shuddering sight to never more
> return that show of blacken'd mutilated corpses!
> That hell unpent and raid of blood, fit for wild tigers
> or for lop-tongued wolves, not reasoning men...
> "Song of the Exposition"

A

In December of 1861, eight months after the beginning of the Civil War, while looking through the list of the wounded from Brooklyn in the New York Tribune, Walt Whitman came across the name "First Lieutenant G. W. Whitmore." Whitman knew immediately, although the name was garbled, that this had to be his brother, George Washington Whitman. The newspaper only indicated that George had been wounded: there was no way for Whitman to find out the nature and severity of the wounds. Desperate to find out what had actually happened, Whitman set out, the very next day, with only fifty dollars in his pocket, to find his brother. Since most of the wounded in those early battles of the Civil War were being treated in hospitals in the nation's capital, he first went to Washington, D.C. On his way to Washington, while changing trains in Philadelphia, his pocket was picked, and he arrived in the nation's capital with "not even a dime" for food and shelter.

In what he described as "the greatest suffering I ever experienced in my life," he frantically searched the hospitals of Washington for some information, some sign about George, "Walking all day and night, unable to ride, trying to get information, trying to get access to big people, &c – I could not get the least clue to anything." Then, quite by accident, he ran into two friends he had made in Boston, while publishing the 1960 edition of Leaves of Grass. They were William O' Connor who was then clerk of the Light House Board in Washington, and Charles Eldridge, who was then assistant to the Army Pay Master. The two friends lent him money and cut through some red tape to enable him to get a military pass to journey to Falmouth, Virginia, where George's regiment was regrouping.

When Whitman arrived at the staging area of the 51st New York, George's unit, he discovered that his brother was only superficially wounded. He remained in the camp for eight days, living the life of a soldier. In those eight days he was introduced to the horrors of war. He tells of his experiences about the search for his brother, in a long letter to his mother, and then continues,

> When I found dear brother George, and found that he was alive and well, O you may imagine how trifling all my little cares and difficulties seemed— they vanished into nothing. And now that I have lived for eight or nine days amid such scenes as the camps furnish, and had a practical part in it all, and realize the way hundreds of thousands of good men

are now living, and have had to live for a year or more, not only without any of the comforts, but with death and sickness and hard marching and hard fighting (and no success at that) for their continual experience – really nothing we call trouble seems worth talking about. One of the first things that met my eyes in a camp was a heap of feet, arms, legs, etc., under a tree in front of a hospital, the Lacy House.

That "heap of feet, arms, legs, etc., under a tree in front of a hospital," that vision of mutilated human flesh, resulting from a terrible battle, and a terrible war, remained with him for the rest of his life.

B

After his eight days at the front, Walt Whitman returned to Washington and remained there throughout the war. He was never to return to Brooklyn except to visit again. During the war years he spent almost all of his spare time, while doing odd jobs to make a living, visiting wounded and dying soldiers, both North and South, in the many military hospitals then located in the nation's capital. Sometimes he would give the soldiers small gifts like candy or oranges, or pencils and paper. Sometimes he would play games with his "boys," like twenty questions, or recite from the soliloquies of Shakespeare. And sometimes he would write letters for them, or agree to write their folks if they died. Or he might just hold their hands, or hold them in his arms if they were frightened or in pain. But most of all he gave them friendship and affection. Most of all he gave himself. He became, in fact, what he had proclaimed in his poems several years earlier:

> Behold I do not give lectures or a little charity,
> When I give I give myself.

Walt Whitman's experiences in the hospitals were chronicled in a diary he kept through the war years, and which he later published in <u>Specimen Days</u>. Whitman estimated that he made 600 trips to the hospitals between 1862 and 1965 and that he visited between 80,000 and 100,000 soldiers. One such visit, as recorded in <u>Specimen Days</u>, can serve as an example of this aspect of Whitman's life.

> This afternoon, July 22, 1863, I spent a long time with a young man I have been with considerable, named Oscar F Wilber, Company G, 154th New York, low with chronic diarrhea and a bad wound also. He asked me to read him a chapter in the New Testament. I complied and asked him what I should read. He said, "Make you own choice." I opened at the close of one of the first books of the evangelists, and read the chapters describing the latter hours of Christ and the scenes at the crucifixion. The poor wasted young man ask'd me to read the following chapter also, how Christ rose again. I read very slowly, for Oscar was feeble. It pleased him very much, yet the tears were in his eyes. He asked me if I enjoyed religion. I said, "Perhaps not, my dear, in the way you mean, and yet may-be it is the same thing." He said, "It is my chief reliance." He talk'd of death, and said he did not fear it. I said, "Why Oscar, don't you think you will get well:" He said, "I may, but it is not probable." He spoke calmly of his condition. The wound was very bad; it discharg'd much. Then the diarrhea had prostrated him, and I felt that he was even then the same as

dying. He behaved very manly and affectionate. The kiss I gave him as I was about leaving, he return'd fourfold. He gave me his mother's address, Mrs. Sally D. Wilber, Allegheny post-office, Cattaraugus County, N.Y. I had several such interviews with him. He died a few days after the one just described.

Whitman gave so much of himself during those war years, spent so much time and exposed himself to so many illnesses, that by war's end he was a sick man himself. He went into the war years in robust health, proud of the condition of his body. He came out of the war years in ill health, facing a stroke, and, most importantly of all, facing the decline of his poetic powers. It may not be an exaggeration to say that Walt Whitman was as much a casualty of the war as any of the soldiers he had ministered to and loved.

C

A year after he went to Virginia and found his brother, a year after he saw that "heap of feet, arms, legs, etc.," a year in which he had confronted much suffering, and dying, Whitman noted, again in a letter to his mother, dated September 8, 1863:

> Mother, one's heart grows sick of war, after all, when you see what it really is; every once in a while I feel so horrified and disgusted – it seems to me like a great slaughterhouse and the men mutually butchering each other – then I feel how impossible it appears, again, to retire from this contest, until we have carried our points (it is cruel to be so tossed from pillar to post in one's judgment.)

> This letter reveals Walt Whitman's growing ambivalence about the Civil War. On the one hand, he had experienced the horror, the suffering, and the death of war, and seen, for himself, what war "really" is. Whitman yearns for the time when the carnage will cease. On the other hand, however, he loves the union, feels the imperative need for its preservation, and feels the war must be pursued, and must succeed, regardless of the carnage, until the integrity of the union is once again restored. To understand Walt Whitman, one needs to understand this sense of ambivalence, this sense of being "tossed from pillar to post."

The Civil War had become the crucial event in his life. Toward the end of his life, Whitman was to say in reference to the war years, and especially his hospital visits, "Without those three or four years and the experiences they gave, 'Leaves of Grass' would not now be existing." Whitman scholars are not quite sure just exactly what Whitman meant by that, but they are sure of the impact the war had on the poet.

Walt Whitman's poems about he war years, and about his hospital ministry, are collected together, in <u>Leaves of Grass</u>, under the heading "Drum Taps." Some of the poems in "Drum Taps" were written before the war, as the war clouds were gathering over the American republic. Others were written in the midst of the war. And still others were written as the war was coming to an end, and after it was over. There is a progression in Whitman's thoughts over those years; a progression which reflects the ambivalence mentioned earlier, a progression which moves from a naïve romanticism to a more honest and realistic view of war.

The Civil War began with the bombardment of Fort Sumter, on April 12, 1861. Walt Whitman had attended the opera in New York, that evening when he heard the newsboys shouting "extra, extra," announcing the terrible news. His hopes, like the hopes of many other Americans, were indelibly linked with the preservation of the union. He was furious with the south for taking action that would threaten the union, and even more furious with northern politicians who had let such a thing come to pass.

Whitman was, at the beginning of the war, what today we might call a "hawk." He welcomed the war and urged the nation "to begin this red business." "Drum Taps" has many passages that glorify war, and the war. He exhibits a martial spirit: "How good they look as they tramp down to the river, sweaty, with their guns on their shoulders." "No longer let our children deem us riches and peace alone," he sings, "We may be terror and carnage, and are so now." "War! An arm'd race is advancing! The welcome for battle, no turning away;" he proclaims, "War! Be it weeks, months, or years, an arm'd race is advancing to welcome it." His little poem titled "to a certain civilian, found in "Drum Taps," underscores the point:

> Did you ask dulcet rhymes from me?
> Did you seek the civilian's peaceful and languishing rhymes?
> Did you find what I sang ere while so hard to follow?
> Why I was not singing erewhile for you to follow, to understand – nor am I now;
> (I have been born of the same as the war was born, the drum-corps rattle is ever to me sweet music, I love well the martial dirge,

> With slow wail and convulsive throb leading the officer's funeral;)
>
> What to such as you anyhow such a poet as I? therefore leave my works,
> And go lull yourself with what you can understand, and with piano-tunes.
> For I lull nobody, and you will never understand me.

The <u>American Heritage Dictionary</u> defines "dulcet" in such terms as: "pleasing to the ear," "quieting," "gently melodious," and "sweet to the taste." What Walt Whitman is saying in this poem, as the nation enters a terrible war, is that he is not going to sing the sweet songs of peace, he is going to sing the terrible songs of war. He is going to write marching music. He is going to sing martial hymns. He is not going to lull people by pretty tunes, he is going to inspire them to fight. "In peace I chanted peace, but now the drum of war is mine," he wrote, "War, red war is my song through your street, O city," Whitman welcomed the war as a kind of moral imperative, as a tonic for the national spirit.

D

Some of the greatest poems about warfare in the English language are found in "Drum Taps." Some of the poems paint exquisite word pictures of events in the war that have the effect of enabling the reader to visualize the scene, of enabling the reader to "be there." One example of these exquisite word pictures is "A March in The Ranks."

> A march in the ranks hard-prest, and the road unknown,

A route through a heavy wood with muffled steps in
    the darkness,
Our army foil'd with loss severe, and the sullen
    remnant retreating,
Till after midnight glimmer upon us the lights of a
    dim-lighted building,
We come to an open space in the woods, and halt by
    the dim-lighted building,
'Tis a large old church at the crossing roads, now an
    impromptu hospital,

Entering but for a minute I see a sight beyond all
    the pictures and poems ever made,
Shadows of deepest, deepest black, just lit by
    moving candles and lamps,
And by one great pitchy torch stationary with wild
    red flame and clouds of smoke,
By these, crowds, groups of forms vaguely I see on
    the floor, some in the pews laid down,
At my feet more distinctly a soldier, a mere lad, in
    danger of bleeding to death, (he is shot in the
    abdomen),
I stanch the blood temporarily, (the youngster's face
    is white as a lily,)
Then before I depart I sweep my eyes o'er the scene
    fain to absorb it all,
Faces, varieties, postures beyond description, most
    in obscurity, some of them dead.
Surgeons operating, attendants holding lights, the
    smell of ether, the odor of blood
The crowd, O the crowd of the bloody forms, the
    yard outside also fill'd,
Some on the bare ground, some on planks or
    stretchers, some in the death-spasm sweating,

> An occasional scream or cry, the doctor's shouted orders or calls,
> The glisten of the little steel instruments catching the glint of the torches,
> These I resume as I chant, I see again the forms, I smell the odor,
> Then hear outside the orders given, Fall in, my men, fall in;
> But first I bend to the dying lad, his eyes open, a half smile gives he me,
> Then the eyes close, calmly close, and I speed forth to the darkness,
> Resuming, marching, ever in darkness marching, on in the ranks,
> The unknown road still marching.

As one reads this poem, and ponders over it, one does get an exquisite word picture of a war scene, one does feel as if one were viewing the scene. But as the picture sinks in, it appears as if the poet is also viewing the scene and not really much a part of it. It is as if the poet is standing off a bit, as if he is some distance from and, except for a moment, now and then, not deeply involved with it. There is a kind of abstraction to the "I"; a sense of "I" as only a poetic device; a kind of disinterested objectivity.

"A Sight in Camp" is equally intense, and equally powerful as a word picture, but there is a different emphasis to it.

> A sight in camp in the daybreak gray and dim,
> As from my tent I emerge so early sleepless,
> As slow I walk in the cool fresh air the path near the hospital tent,
> Three forms I see on stretchers lying, brought out there untended lying,

Over each the blanket spread, ample brownish
  woolen blanket,
Gray and heavy blanket, covering all.

Curiously I halt and silent stand,
Then with light fingers I from the face of the nearest
  the first just lift the blanket;
Who are you elderly man so gaunt and grim, with
  well-grey'd hair, and flesh all sunken about the
  eyes?
Who are you my dear comrade?

Then to the second I step – and who are you my
  child and darling?
Who are you sweet boy with cheeks yet blooming?

Then to the third – a face nor child nor old, very
  calm, as of beautiful yellow-white ivory;
Young man I think I know you – I think this face is
  the face of the Christ himself,
Dead and divine and brother of all, and here again
  he lies.

Both poems are very fine word pictures, but there is a qualitative difference between "A March in the Ranks" and "A Sight in Camp" – a difference which can be defined in terms of sensitivity and intense intimacy. Whereas the first has an objective quality, the second is more subjective. In the second poem the poet comes into contact, not with soldiers, but with a human being – a human being to love.

It was intrinsic to Whitman's poetics that he deal as much as possible with concrete things, and especially with concrete human beings. In his earliest poems he envisioned himself as the great lover, the great lover of flesh and blood human beings. In the poems which reflect the early part of the war, however, he tended to see human beings not as people, but as part of a great national struggle over principles. What Whitman discovered in Washington during the war years, was the human face of war. The casualties in a war are real flesh and blood people. Whitman not only nursed the young soldiers in the hospitals of Washington, he loved them. And he saw his loved ones suffer and die. The poet is to become their voice. The martial spirit is gone. Soldiers are no longer just soldiers, they are now brothers.

E

That "heap of feet, arms, legs, etc." that he saw in Virginia, the pain and the suffering that he saw in the military hospitals, and the deaths of so many young men that he had come to love, changed his whole way of looking at war. That profound change in his life is highlighted in what may be one of the major theme poems of "Drum Taps," "The Wound Dresser," in which he reflects on his hospital stays,

> (Arous'd and angry, I'd thought to beat the alarum,
>   and urge relentless War
> But soon my fingers fail'd me, my face droop'd and
>   I resign'd myself,
> To sit by the wounded and soothe them, or silently
>   watch the dead;....)

That profound change in his life is expressed in another poem, written as the war came to an end, a poem appropriately called "Reconciliation."

> Word over all, beautiful as the sky,

> Beautiful that war and all its deeds of carnage must in time be utterly lost,
>
> That the hands of the sisters Death and Night incessantly softly wash again, and ever again, this soil'd world;
> For my enemy is dead, a man divine as myself is dead,
> I look where he lies white-faced and still in the coffin – I draw near,
> Bend down and touch lightly with my lips the white face in the coffin.

And it finds its most complete expression, perhaps, when he is an older man, in his "Song of The Exposition:"

> Away with themes of war! Away with war itself! Hence from my shuddering sight to never more return that show of blacken'd mutilated corpses!
> The hell unpent and raid of blood, fit for wild tigers or for lop-tongued wolves, not reasoning men....,

Or in "Autumn Rivulets," written near the end of his life,

> When late I sang sad was my voice
> Sad where the shows around me with deafening noises of hatred and smoke of war;
> In the midst of the conflict, the heroes, I stood,
> Or pass'd with slow step through the wounded and dying,
> But now I sing not war,
> Nor the measur'd march of soldiers, nor the tents of camps,

> Nor the regiments hastily coming up deploying in line of battle;
> No more the sad, unnatural shows of war.

F

There is a sense in which the "Drum Taps" poems provide a culmination for the poems which Walt Whitman called "Calamus." The "Calamus" poems celebrate love between men, the love of comrades. In "Calamus" Whitman sees himself as the poet "who was not proud of his songs, but of the measureless ocean of love within him, and freely pour'd it forth." "Who but I should understand lovers and all their sorrow and joy?" he sings, "And who but I should be the poet of comrades?" After his experiences in the Washington hospitals, Whitman, once again was a poet who poured out "measureless oceans of love," who became the poet of comrades and lovers. And in the process uttered a new vision for the republic:

> Over the carnage rose prophetic a voice,
> Be not dishearten'd, affection shall solve the problems of freedom yet,
> Those who love each other shall become invincible.

"Were you looking to be held together by lawyers? Or by an agreement on a paper? or by arms?" he asks, "Nay, nor the world, nor any living thing, will so cohere." What will make the world, or any living thing cohere? What will make the world hold together? His answer is love.

> Come, I will make the continent indissoluble,
> I will make the most splendid race the sun ever shone upon,

> I will make divine magnetic lands,
> With the love of comrades,
> With the life-long love of comrades.

One may be inclined to feel that there is a certain naiveté in this, but it is that same answer all of the great religions have given across all of the centuries. As the "Tao Te Ching" puts it:

> The loving are the victorious.
> Love resists and conquers all.
> Heaven arms with love
> Those it would not see destroyed.

In the prophetic vision of Walt Whitman "the life long love of comrades" will bring an end to war. The poet has known war and the death, the misery and the destruction that it brings. He now knows that any religion appropriate for a new world will have to recognize the foolishness of war and will have to work to create a nation and a world at peace.

CHAPTER XII
SCIENCE, TO YOU THE FIRST HONORS ALWAYS

I accept reality and dare not question it,
Materialism first and last imbuing.

Hurrah for positive Science!
Long live exact demonstration!

Gentlemen, to you the first honors always!
Your facts are useful, and yet they are not my dwelling,
I but enter by them to an area of my dwelling.
                     "Song of Myself"

Walter Whitman was born on Long Island in New York, in what is now Huntington Station, on May 31, 1819. When he was four, his father, who was an unsuccessful house builder, moved his family to Brooklyn and it was in Brooklyn that Walt grew up. Walt Whitman's family was poor so he had little of what is usually called a "formal education." He went to grammar school from the age of six to the age of eleven and then went to work as an office boy, first in a law office and then in a doctor's office.

From the time he was twelve until he was seventeen he worked in various printing offices, learning the printing trade and becoming a journeyman printer. After a couple of years of teaching school, he became editor of a succession of Brooklyn and New York newspapers. When he wasn't working as a printer, or as a teacher, or as an editor, he worked, from time to time, as unsuccessfully as his father, at the house building business.

Information such as this illustrates the fact that Walt Whitman did not have the background usually associated with nineteenth century intellectuals. He did not come from a prominent family. He did not go to Harvard or Yale. He did not have extensive opportunities, as a young person, to travel. His education came about through the experience of living. He was fortunate, as a boy of eleven in that law office, when one of the lawyers took a special liking to him and purchased for him a subscription to a revolving library. From that time forward, throughout his life, he was an avid reader. He was also fortunate, at a young age, to work for newspaper offices. Tickets were always available to news people to cultural events and from a very young age Whitman would attend the symphony, the opera, stage plays and other similar events in the performing arts.

Whitman was also fortunate in living near New York City, then as now the greatest city in the new world: a city, even then, of a million or more people. Visitors from all over the world would come to New York City – artists, performers, government officials, and the great professors. In New York he had a great number of museums and lecture halls to visit and he visited them all. One of his favorite places in New York was a private museum dedicated to the artifacts of ancient Egypt and young Walt Whitman spent hours marveling at such a glorious human past and learning from the curator of that museum. Walt Whitman had no formal education but there was in New York, and in Brooklyn and in the rural nature of Long Island a kind of university that was particularly suited to Walt Whitman's kind of mind.

There are at least two things about Whitman's mind that may be necessary for an understanding of his life and of his ideas. The first of these was an insatiable curiosity. He was curious about anything and everything. He loved the opera, as I mentioned, and felt it played an important role in the development of his poetry. But he also loved the great omnibuses that carried people down Broadway, in New York, and often could be seen trying his hand at handling the teams of horses. He was equally at home observing and trying to understand the upper classes of New York as he was the lower classes, of prostitutes as well as bankers. He loved to walk on the shores of Long Island and to identify the various forms of life – plants and animals – he found there. In books he was curious about all kinds of things: strange places and strange customs and strange ideas.

But not only was he curious about anything and everything, he had the amazing capacity of absorbing it all, making it part of his memory. No one can read <u>Leaves of Grass</u> without noticing, as most students of Walt Whitman have noticed, this capacity to take in, and store, every observation, every experience. His mind seemed to be like a funnel which carried into his collective memory everything he came across.

One of the many things Walt Whitman was curious about was the rapidly expanding field of science. The period of his lifetime, which spanned the larger part of the nineteenth century, was a time of great advances in scientific understanding. Walt Whitman, in his youth and as an adult, read everything he could get his hands on about astronomy and geology and physics and biology, and attended many lectures in New York City on such subjects. He hungrily absorbed knowledge from those areas and incorporated all of them into his poetry. Those who have studied his poetry with special reference to his scientific understanding have marveled at how accurately, at least in terms of the knowledge of his day, his poetry reflects scientific thought. "That Whitman possessed no trained scientific instinct is unquestionably true," Havelock Ellis noted in <u>The New Spirit</u>,

> But it is impossible to estimate his significance without understanding what he owes to science. ....
> He was indebted to those scientific conceptions which, like Emerson, he had absorbed or divined.

Walt Whitman was not just curious about science, however, he found it necessary to incorporate the insights gained from the scientific enterprise into his prophetic vision, into his construct of a greater religion. The word "science," which is this context refers more accurately to fundamental knowledge than it does to technology, is not something separate from religion but part of a single process shared by both religion and science. Both share a commitment to the same truth.

B

Whitman's nineteenth century world was one characterized by the rise of science, by the increase in knowledge about the natural world and the natural universe. Such scientific understanding arose out of the past, found living expression in his present, and had to be incorporated into his vision of the future. No religion, no prophetic vision, has authenticity, has validity, Whitman felt, which does not recognize this reality. Such a perspective is reiterated many times in his various prose works.

[Great poetry] "must in no respect ignore science or the modern, but inspire itself with science and the modern," he wrote in Democratic Vistas, a prose essay written in the middle of his career. [Great poetry], he went on, "must bend its vision toward the future, more than the past." "Whatever may have been the case in years gone by," he added in one of his prefaces, "A Backward Glance O'er Travel'd Roads," this one written near the end of his career,

> The true use for the imaginative faculty of modern times is to give ultimate vivification to facts, to science, and to common lives, endowing them with glows and glories and final illustriousness which belongs to every real thing, and to real things only.

Whitman cannot express his case in clearer or stronger terms. The role of the poet – the role of the prophet, the role of religion – is to deal with the real world, the natural world as revealed through the emerging processes of science. The poet/prophet is called upon to take that world and to make it sacred, to enclose it with meaning, and to make it alive in such a way that human beings could find their own aliveness in it. Others, in their own day, in the past, used their imaginations to come up with constructs of meaning that spoke to their time. So can people in the present time. It was the task of the true poets of his generation, the true prophets, Whitman felt, to use their knowledge of the world to generate grand epics that can give the human heart hope and courage and faith.

The modern world can not hope to achieve what the past achieved, in past worlds, without faithfulness to science, without faithfulness to reality, without faithfulness to the real world as moderns know it to be. The world needs and the world awaits the time when poets and religionists take up this perspective, as Whitman put it in <u>Democratic Vistas</u>:

> The highest and subtlest and broadest truths of modern science wait for their true assignment and last vivid flashes of light—as Democracy waits for its—through first class metaphysicians and philosophs.

What Whitman could see in his nineteenth century world, as we can see in our twenty first century world, is a continuing condition of conflict between religion and science. Science has opened vast new opportunities to understand the universe in which human beings live and yet religions tend to tenaciously hang on to doctrines that seem to contradict those opportunities. "Note today, a curious spectacle and conflict," Whitman wrote in <u>Democratic Vistas</u>:

> Science testing absolutely all thoughts, all works, has already burst well upon the world – a sun, mounting, most illuminating, most glorious -- surely never again to set. But against it, deeply entrenched, holding possession, yet remains (not only through the churches and schools but by unimaginative literature and unregenerate poetry) the fossil theory of the mythic-materialistic, superstitious, untaught and credulous, fable loving, primitive ages of humanity.

Science is certainly here to stay and yet religion has not caught up with that fact and has not really begun to incorporate it into a contemporary religious view of the universe. What is needed, Whitman felt, are poet/prophets who will capture the essence of this exciting and emerging world and recast it in lyrics which will speak to the human soul. As Whitman says in <u>Democratic Vistas</u>:

> America needs, and the world needs, a class of bards who will, now and ever, so link and tally the rational physical being of man, with the ensembles of time and space, and with the vast and uniform show, Nature.

C

Walt Whitman incorporates his theory of the proper relationships between science and religion in the modern world in the poetry of <u>Leaves of Grass</u>. The reader should notice a difference in tone in the poetry. In the prose passages discussed above, Whitman refers, in the second person, to "the poet" or the prophet. In his poetry he takes on the first person identity of the prophet. It is no longer "the poet says this or that;" it is now an "I." "I say!"

In his first preface, Whitman says of "the poet:" "he is no arguer, he is judgment." What he means by that is that the poet/prophet, like the prophets of the past, is to speak with authority, to pronounce judgment, to proclaim the Truth. His heroes clearly are the Old Testament prophets who prefaced their pronouncements with "Thus saith the Lord." In his poetry Whitman assumes this prophetic role. It is this spirit of prophecy one finds in <u>Leaves of Grass</u>.

Whitman deals as a prophet most powerfully on the theme of science and religion in "Song of Myself."

> I accept time absolutely.
> I accept reality and dare not question it,
> Materialism first and last imbuing.

To understand this passage, one needs to clearly understand what Whitman means by the word "materialism." He does not mean the mania for owning things, which is the common, contemporary, use of the word. He is referring to a philosophical concept which the American Heritage Dictionary defines as "the philosophical opinion that physical matter in its movements and modifications is the only reality and that everything in the universe, including thought, feeling, mind and will, can be explained in terms of physical laws." Walt Whitman is a "materialist." The poet constantly says that he will make his poems out of things, out of objects, out of reality.

What Whitman is saying in these lines is that it is time that matters; it is reality that matters; it is the physical world that matters. He will not predicate his prophetic vision on that which is not real and is not located in time. There is a sense here that "what you see is what you get;" that the real world – the world which we see with our eyes, hear with our ears, touch with our fingers, interact with our bodies – is the ultimate world. And it is the same things which are sacred; the same things which are the proper sphere of religion.

Whitman's most powerful affirmations on this score is found in his poem, "I Sing the Body Electric." "If anything is sacred," he says, "The human body is sacred." It is not some abstract spirit, nor some abstract soul, that is sacred. It is this body, this reality, this physical being that is sacred.

Walt Whitman is very emphatic on this point, I suppose, because he wants to make it very clear that religious truth is not found on some other path than on the one science takes. They both take the same path and both search for the same kind of truth. They are not in opposition to each other.

"Hurrah for positive science! Long live exact demonstration!" Whitman goes on to say in "Song of Myself," "Gentlemen, to you the first honors always!" Once again, perhaps a definition would help in understanding at this point. What exactly does the poet mean by the word "first" and by the phrase "first honors?" It needs to be clear that he does not mean the "highest" – that honor, for Whitman always goes to the "true poet," to the prophet. By "first" he means the "initial honors;" by "first" he means the place one starts. In religion one must begin with "positive science." One must begin with "exact demonstration." One must begin with a fundamental respect for truths the scientists discover.

The function of the scientist, in Whitman's scheme of things, is to explore the physical universe: to study nature, to study the cosmos, and to arrive at deeper and more profound understandings of the nature of things. There is a sense here of "let scientists be scientists" and let religion honor their work and not be afraid to accept the truths they discover. A religion for the modern world does not need propaganda: it needs the insights science can reveal.

"Your facts are useful, and yet they are not my dwelling," Whitman concludes in "Song of Myself," "I but enter by them to an area of my dwelling." In these two lines are found the very heart, from Walt Whitman's perspective, of the proper relationship between religion and science in the modern world. The place of the poet – the prophet, the theologian – is not the same place as that of the scientist, but the poet/prophet enters to his or her place through the place of the scientist.

Although the poet begins with that which science demonstrates – with facts and with knowledge – the poet does not end there. The poet takes the knowledge of the world and of the universe which science offers, respects it, uses it, honors it, is faithful to it, but moves through and beyond it to a more adequate religious vision for the world and for the human race.

The poet or the prophet is ultimately concerned with spiritual things rather than with the material things which are the domain of the scientist. The poet/prophet is ultimately concerned with the soul whereas the scientist is concerned with the body. But one can approach an honest spirituality, and an honest concept of soul, only by accepting the physical and material world and by moving through it and beyond it.

"The known universe has one complete lover and that is the greatest of poets," Whitman says in his preface to the first edition of <u>Leaves of Grass</u>. "The greatest of poets," the authentic prophet of religion for the modern world, he is saying, must have a love affair with the real world, or, as he says elsewhere, "with the ensembles of time and space, and with the vast and multiform show, Nature."

D

A greater religion, a religion adequate for the modern world, has to give science the "first honors." To be valid, religion has to go through the "dwelling" of science to find its own proper dwelling. Because religion has not, over the past couple of centuries, maintained an honest regard for science, it has become not only obsolete, it has become fundamentally irrelevant as well.

There was a time when theology, the study of religion, was known as the "Queen Science;" a time when the study of religion had an honored and respected place. In the modern world it has now been reduced to a place where it rates only a footnote; a place where nobody is interested in theology except the theologians. There was a time when "metaphysics" was a valued part of academic curriculums and intellectual discourse, but that was a long time ago. It has become, at best a curious anachronism and at worst, a laughing matter. Metaphysics which once could be defined, honorably, as "the philosophical study of first principles or of ultimate reality" – the domain of religion – has degenerated into superstition, absurd ideas, and downright quackery.

The failure of religion to come to honest terms with science, furthermore, has produced, over the past decades and even centuries, a chronic state of intellectual schizophrenia. Truth depends upon perspective and that which goes under the rubric "religious truth" is separate from, alien to, and incompatible with, that which goes under the rubric "scientific truth." One can only be scientific with half of themselves, or religious with half of themselves, and not find a sense of wholeness in that which can be called <u>The Truth</u>.

The failure of religion to come to honest terms with science, still further, has led to the rise of all kinds of pseudo-sciences in the twentieth century which can only be seen as evolving out of fear of that which science reveals. The pseudo-science known as "creationism" is perhaps the best example of this, but the temptations to form pseudo-scientific movements is found everywhere. The intellectual schizophrenia it produces is epidemic.

Frederick Neitsche once wrote: "If you wish to strive for peace of mind, then believe, if you wish to be a devotee of truth, then inquire." Neitsche was making a commentary on the deep split between conventional religion and the knowledge of the universe which is at the root of what we call "science." There is a great deal of validity in that thought. The science of the modern world does demand "inquiry." But "believing" and "inquiring" do not need to be mutually exclusive. Religion and science do not need to be antagonists.

Whitman can show us a way out of this impasse. Walt Whitman can help us to understand religion both in terms of "inquiry" and in terms of "believing." Religion can once again make some claims to validity if it will go about its task after going through the dwelling of science. Science and religion are not the same thing but they deal with the same truth. One deals with the nature of things and the other with the meaning of things, but they both should deal with the same things. For both religion and science, as they go about their respective tasks in the modern world, and play their respective roles, it must be the truth that is the object of faith for both, and the focal point of commitment. Two thousand years ago a prophet by the name of Jesus said: "You shall know the truth and the truth shall make you free." If religion in the twenty-first century commits itself to knowing the truth – the same truth, that is, that science commits itself to knowing – it may discover that it shall be set free, indeed!

CHAPTER XIII
THE TRUTHS OF THE EARTH CONTINUALLY WAIT

> I swear there is no greatness or power that does not emulate those of the earth,
> There can be no theory of any account unless it corroborate the theory of the earth,
> No politics, song, religion, behavior, or what not, is of account, unless it compare with the amplitude of the earth,
> Unless it face the exactness, vitality, impartiality, rectitude of the earth.
>
> "Song of the Rolling Earth"

A

There are a few moments in the life of a people, or an era, that are of such import as to alter forever the way people will see themselves and their world. One of those momentous events of the 20th century, in a century where the momentous is most often characterized by horrible wars, was the Apollo flights to the moon. For the first time, in all of time, human beings have seen the earth whole. This planet which, over eons of time has shaped and molded us and our existence, was seen from outside of its own frame of reference, as if a stranger might see our house when coming to visit us for the very first time. Only a few astronauts actually experienced, first hand, that view of earth from space, but through the marvel of photography, the whole human race can see the earth as it truly is.

That view of the earth from outer space is reshaping the way we look at the earth and the way we look at human beings on the earth. We now know that the earth is blue and beautiful, but we expected that. We did not expect the earth to be so "fragile" and "vulnerable."

The very thought of trying to save a fragile and vulnerable earth is a new thought to the human species. It was the earth that took care of us. To think in terms of our caring for the world, of preserving its existence, was truly a new thought under the sun. Every time and every culture has had its own way of looking at the world and of conceptualizing the human place in it, but that new view of our small, blue, beautiful planet has required us, and is requiring us, to shape a new image of ourselves and a new image of earth.

B

Walt Whitman's world, the America of the nineteenth century, was also no stranger to momentous events. Walt Whitman responded to the momentous events of his time and tried to describe their meaning for the nation and for the human race. That is the intent of one of his last great poems, "Passage to India," which was first published in 1870. "Passage to India" was written to commemorate three great social and engineering achievements of the decade of the civil war: the Union Pacific Railroad, the Atlantic Cable, and the Suez Canal.

These three events were destined to change the shape of the world and the shape of history. The Union Pacific Railroad, which was completed in 1860, connected the east coast of the United States with the west coast, providing for much more rapid and complete communication between the two parts of the new world. The Atlantic cable, which was laid in 1866, provided for almost instantaneous communication between America and England and, by extension, with the whole of the European continent. The Suez Canal, completed in 1869, connected Europe with Asia, and symbolized, for Walt Whitman, the uniting of the East with the West.

Walt Whitman saw these three great events as radically altering the way human beings could understand the world and their own place in it. After the two halves of the continent were linked together; after America was connected with Europe; and after the western world was connected to the eastern world: a new world view would have to emerge. That new worldview will require a new religious understanding, and will require the songs of a new prophet:

> After the seas are all cross'd, (as they seem already cross'd)
> After the great captains and engineers have accomplish'd their work,
> After the noble inventors, after the scientists, the chemist, the geologist, the ethnologist,
> Finally shall the poet worthy the name,
> The true Son of God shall come singing his songs.

One of the songs the "true Son of God" will have to sing in this new world, is the song of the earth. Walt Whitman could not see the earth as we see it now, from outer space, but he did "see" the earth as well as any man could have in the nineteenth century. There is a powerful passage describing the earth in "Passage to India" which seems almost contemporary in thought. "O vast Rondure, swimming in space," he writes, "Now first it seems my thoughts begin to span thee." I expect that Whitman chose the word "Rondure," rather than "orb" or "sphere," because of its connotations of beauty and grace.

Walt Whitman would also have understood how that view of the earth from outer space could alter one's perception of the world. He was convinced, in fact, that a radical change in the perception of the world was occurring in his own time. There is both a new worldview forming, and "hints and clews" about how that new view of earth would shape religion in the modern world expressed in a poem first published in 1856. The poem is called "The Song of The Rolling Earth," and begins with these words:

> A song of the rolling earth, and of words according,
> Were you thinking that those were the words, those
>   upright lines? Those curves, angles, dots?
> No those are not the words, the substantial words
>   are in the ground and sea,
> They are in the air, they are in you.

Whitman is suggesting two very important things in these opening words from "Song of the Rolling Earth."

In the first place, in thinking of "words," Whitman is expressing an idea that lies at the very core of his theory of poetry. Words, what he here calls the "substantial words," are always found in things. These "upright lines, curves, angles, dots" are but a system for indicating the substantial words. If we do not experience the reality which the words express, we miss the "true" words. The authentic poet for the modern world, from Whitman's perspective, will use the printed word only as a symbol system to specify concrete things.

In the second place, and this is the theme of "A Song of the Rolling Earth," the most "substantial words," the most solid and meaningful words, are found in the "apple shaped earth and we upon it." They are found in the "ground and in the sea" and in the "you" and the "me" that live on this rolling earth. "Human bodies are words, myriads of words," he goes on, "Air, soil, water, fire—those are words." We miss the meaning of the "Song of the Rolling Earth" if we do not see behind his words the most fundamental reality, the most substantial reality we can know, the earth and we ourselves upon it. These are the words that give the form, the substance, and the meaning to human life. "I swear I begin to see little or nothing in audible words," Whitman writes,

> All merges toward the presentation of the unspoken meanings of the earth,
> Toward him who sings the songs of the body and of the truths of the earth,
> Toward him who makes the dictionaries of words that print cannot touch.

From the perspective of the prophetic vision of Walt Whitman, human beings are not going to find ultimate meanings in written words. We will not find the meaning of life in Bibles or in other religious texts, or in the words of religious traditions from the past. We are not even going to find it, Whitman insists, in Leaves of Grass. We will find that meaning only in the context of earth. The earth contains all we need to know. The "great mother," the earth, may be "dumb," that is, she may be unable to speak in our language, but she is "eloquent," that is, she speaks in a more substantial language. We need to listen to her speak in her own language, need to take her own values into our own being, and become faithful to her substantial reality.

It is not too much to say that, for Walt Whitman, the earth, itself, is the greatest of poems. It is not too much to say that a central theme in the prophetic vision of Walt Whitman is a celebration of the earth. It is not too much to say that, for Whitman, a central task of the poet/prophet is to sing the praises of earth. "O truth of the earth!" Whitman wrote in an unused line, "I am determin'd to press my way toward you." "Who has made hymns fit for the earth?" he asks in "Excelsior," "I am mad with devouring ecstasy to make joyous hymns for the whole earth." It is clear, as he proclaims in "Song of Myself," Walt Whitman is in love with the earth:

> Smile O voluptuous cool-breath'd earth!
> Earth of slumbering and liquid trees!
> Earth of departed sunset – earth of the mountains misty-topt!
> Earth of the vitreous pour of the full moon just tinged with blue!
> Earth of shine and dark mottling the tide of the river!
> Earth of the limpid gray of clouds brighter and clearer for my sake!
> Far-swooping elbow'd earth – rich apple-blossom'd earth!
> Smile, for your lover comes.

C

"The earth does not exhibit itself nor refuse to exhibit itself," Walt Whitman says in some indicative words from "Song of the Rolling Earth:"

> The earth does not argue,
> Is not pathetic, has no arrangements,
> Does not scream, haste, persuade, threaten, promise,
> Makes no discriminations, has no conceivable failures,
> Closes nothing, refuses nothing, shuts none out,
> Of all the powers, objects, states, it notifies, shuts none out.

What the poet is attempting to suggest by these words is that the earth is absolutely trustworthy. It does not play favorites. It includes all. It cannot betray us. Perhaps we can make this a little clearer by exploring Whitman's use of the word "pathetic." He is probably referring to what is sometimes called, in philosophy, "the pathetic fallacy," which is the attribution of human emotions to things. The earth "is not pathetic:" the earth is not emotional. It does not have moods. It does not act in a capricious manner. The earth is the same for all people. The earth, "tumbling on, dreading nothing," is changeless. Because it is changeless we can trust it, we can rely on it, we can put our faith in it.

"To her children the words of the eloquent dumb great mother never fail," Whitman continues, "The true words do not fail, for motion does not fail and reflection does not fail, Also the day and night do not fail...." The earth does not try to delude us. If we fall off of a tall building, we will hurt ourselves; we will always hurt ourselves. The laws of the earth are solid, secure, and utterly reliable. Because of this attribute of the earth we can always put our confidence in her, whatever changes there might be in life.

To say that the earth does not display an emotional nature, however, is not to say that it is unsupportive of human life. Walt Whitman sees the human being as having come out of the earth and is therefore, by nature, adapted to living on the earth. It is this "cold, impassive earth" which sustains human existence. "The earth does not withhold, it is generous enough," he continues in "Song of the Rolling Earth," "The truths of the earth continually wait, they are not so conceal'd either." What he means is that we have all we need, on this earth, to know our complete humanness. The fundamental truths about what it means to be human await in the earth, they are to be found there. All we have to do is look, and do not have to look very hard at that. The truth about life is to be found in the earth.

"The earth," Whitman writes, "is rude, silent, incomprehensible at first." I understand the poet to be saying that the earth is difficult to "understand" or "know," but I wondered why he chose the word "rude." I wondered how "rude" could be one of the "words" of the earth. I was surprised to discover, in the American Heritage Dictionary, how many and varied were the definitions of "rude:" "primitive and uncivilized;" "unrefined and uncouth;" "crude and rough;" "vigorous and robust;" "harsh and severe." Perhaps all such definitions are contained in Whitman's use of the word, "rude." We cannot approach the earth, and hear her speak, as civilized human beings. She does not speak the language of literary discourse. We have to put aside our refinement, and our sense of propriety, if the "words" of the earth are to be heard. We hear the words of the earth through our "natural" and not through our "cultured" bodies.

The earth is "rude" and "incomprehensible," Whitman writes, but only "at first." If we are patient – "be not discouraged, keep on" – we will discover, in the earth, "divine things more beautiful than words can tell." "How perfect the earth," Whitman says in a rejected line, "and the minutest thing upon it." We can discover that "beauty," that "perfection," that "divinity," only when we permit the earth to speak to us on her own terms.

D

When human beings, through the wonderful invention of photography, were able to see the whole earth for the very first time in the entire history of the human race, it radically changed our understanding of earth. When human beings begin to understand that there may not be any thing else like this earth in the whole vastness of the known cosmos, it becomes difficult to put feelings about the earth into words. One strange word that comes to mind is the word "sacred." Perhaps this small blue sphere, in the dark and cold of space, might be the most sacred thing of all! And now, it seems, this sacred earth must become central to any appropriate religion for the modern world.

A century before the Apollo project, Walt Whitman expressed a very similar thought. For Whitman, as was noted in an earlier chapter, the sacred is to be found in the most concrete. It begins with the concrete individual, therefore, and moves on to the concrete life: life lived in a particular time and place. It is the earth however, the concrete physical earth, that makes both life and the human individual possible. Walt Whitman's theology is constructed out of such stuff as this. In "Song of the Rolling Earth," Whitman defines the poet/prophet for the new world as "him who sings the songs of the body and of the truths of the earth." The poet/prophet is one, he adds in "Kosmos,"

> Who out of the theory of the earth and his or her own body understands by subtle analogy all other theories.

"Those honour Nature well," wrote Pascal, "who teach that she can speak on everything, even on theology." Walt Whitman honored Nature well. The earth, "the great mother," becomes, for Whitman, the center and the focus of his vision of religion. "All merges toward the presentation of the unspoken meanings of the earth," he sings in "Song of the Rolling Earth," in words that seem singularly appropriate for this first decade of the twenty first century:

> I swear there is no greatness or power that does not emulate those of the earth,
> There can be no theory of any account unless it corroborate the theory of the Earth,
> No politics, song, religion, behavior, or what not, is of account, unless it compare with the amplitude of the earth,
> Unless it face the exactness, vitality, impartiality, rectitude of the earth.

It is hard to see how Whitman could have used stronger words to underscore his own conviction about the absolute sacredness of earth. Even the definition of God must "emulate" the earth. Religion and politics, and everything else, must deal with the amplitude, the "fullness," the "greatness" of the earth. No theory is of "any account" unless it deals with the reality of earth. Whitman would have understood the prophetic insight of another prophet of the modern world, Frederich Nietzche:

I conjure you, my brethren, remain faithful to earth, and do not believe those who speak unto you of super terrestrial hopes! Poisoners they are, whether they know it or not.

E

"I swear the earth shall be complete to him or her who shall be complete," Whitman writes in "Song of the Rolling Earth," "The earth remains jagged and broken only to him or her who remains jagged and broken." The earth remains "jagged and broken" for human beings in the modern world because we have set ourselves off from the world of nature. We have seen ourselves, and our meaning, in terms beyond the earth. Religion, in terms of the prophetic vision of Walt Whitman, has to be redefined in the modern world in natural terms. The human being can find spiritual wholeness in the new world only as one embraces the divinity of earth.

There abides in the dominant religion of the western world, in Christianity, however, the notion that the human beings are "in" but not "of" the world. "Earth is our temporary dwelling place," Christianity has proclaimed, "but Heaven is our eternal home." In Leaves of Grass Whitman rejected that idea and proclaimed that we are both "in" and "of" the world. A religion appropriate for the modern world demands that we be faithful to earth. It is the task of the poet/prophet to sing the praises not of God, but of the earth. The "shape of earth divine and wondrous," was, for Whitman, one of his "gods."

"O earth that hast no voice, confide to me a voice," Whitman sings in "The Return of the Heroes,"

> O lavish brown parturient earth –
> O infinite teeming womb,
> A song to narrate thee.

The world requires, as Whitman understood more than a century ago, the formation of a new religion that can underwrite a world view appropriate for the time. An understanding of the sacredness of Earth, as expressed in "Song of the Rolling Earth" and elsewhere in <u>Leaves of Grass</u>, is a central aspect of the prophetic vision of Walt Whitman.

Every time and every culture has had its own way of looking at the world and of conceptualizing the human place in it, as Walt Whitman realized more than a century and a half ago. That view of our small, blue, beautiful planet from outer space is requiring us, once again, to shape a new image of ourselves and a new image of earth.

CHAPTER XIV
NATURE AND HUMANITY DISJOIN'D NO MORE

When the full grown poet came,
Out spake pleased Nature (the round impassive
   globe, with all its shows of day and night,)
   saying, He is mine;
But out spake too the Soul of man, proud, jealous
   and unreconciled, Nay, he is mine alone;
--Then the full-grown poet stood between the two,
   and took each by the hand;
And to-day and ever so stands, as blender, uniter,
   tightly holding hands,
Which he will never release until he reconciles the
   two,
And wholly and joyously blends them.
"Good-bye My Fancy"

A

With the dawning of the nineteenth century, the age of science, the age of industrial technology, the age of the machine – in a word, the modern age – was already in full bloom. William Wordsworth, the great English poet, could see that it posed some very important problems for the human spirit. Already the slums of

London, spawned by the industrial revolution, had become a blot on the human conscience, a terrible affront to human dignity. Wordsworth's world was a war weary world, like our own, and with each new war there was an emergence of new war machines which provided for ever more efficient systems of death and destruction. Materialism – this time in the contemporary sense of the word: the mania for owning things—had already become a part of the human psyche. In this context Wordsworth wrote, in 1807, one of his most powerful, and well know, poems:

> The world is too much with us; late and soon,
> Getting and spending we lay waste our powers:
> Little we see in Nature that is ours;
> We have given our hearts away, a sordid boon!
> The sea that bares her bosom to the moon;
> The winds that will be howling at all hours,
> And are up-gathered now like sleeping flowers;
> For this, for everything, we are out of tune;
> It moves us not. – Great God! I'd rather be
> A pagan suckled in a creed outworn;
> So might I, standing on this pleasant lea,
> Have glimpses that would make me less forlorn;
> Have sight of Proteus rising from the sea;
> Or hear old Triton blow his wreathed horn.

With the dawn of the "Modern age" a new "humanism" had emerged: a Christian humanism, which saw the human being as above, or superior to Nature. The old Biblical adage about "subduing the earth" found expression with new vengeance. Trees were for cutting down, hills were for laying low, rivers were for damming up, and all for the purpose of feeding the insatiable appetite of an industrial society. Nature was seen as an enemy, "red in tooth and claw," something to be conquered. The earth, more and more, was being seen, not as the human home, but as the storehouse of materials out of which the human race could build a superior human home.

The western world in Wordsworth's day, as civilization moved into the 19th century, and continuing down to our own day, saw Nature as little more than as a storehouse containing the resources needed to fuel an ever growing industry. By 1807 the human race—that part of it which occupies the western world at least—was well on its way to becoming a world where the forests were all cut down, where the mountains were all scarred, where the streams were all polluted, where the air was no longer fit to breathe.

Wordsworth could feel as he stood on that pleasant lea, two centuries ago, that the western world was losing contact with Nature and, in the process giving its heart away. A human race divorced from a feeling of kinship with Nature, however much the modern world may have added material blessings to life, is an impoverished race. "Great God!" the poet says, "I'd rather be a pagan in a creed outworn" – "I'd rather have the magic that the primitive person felt about Nature than live in this modern world that is alienated from Nature," Wordsworth seems to be saying, alienated from that which, in another poem, he calls "the heart and soul of all my mortal being."

B

The same theme is picked up by a new world poet, a couple of decades later, Walt Whitman. A clue to their shared perspective is found in the fact that both of them always spelled Nature with a capital "N." Both of them saw Nature as something sacred, that is, as something worthy of reverence and awe.

There is a great deal of difference between the two poets, to be sure. Wordsworth was, in some respect at least, preeminently a Nature poet, a rural poet, a romantic poet. He lived in the country and the preponderance of imagery in his poems reflects the "lake region" which was his home; imagery of hills and valleys, farms and pastures, and visions of the sea. And he was more than a little suspicious of that which could be called "modernity."

Shortly after Wordsworth wrote "The World Is Too Much With Us," bands of workers rioted in the industrial areas of England, destroying textile machinery under the conviction that they were responsible for high unemployment and low wages. The rioting workers, named after a mythical character named Ned Ludd, or "King Ludd," were called Luddites. Over time the word "luddite" came to mean any one who was opposed to progress. It may not be fair or accurate to suggest that Wordsworth was a luddite, but he does seem to long for the "good old days" where one could, presumably, live a happier and more meaningful life. In all of Wordsworth's work there is that romantic view of Nature which sees it in opposition to the lived lives of the modern world.

> One impulse from a vernal wood
> May teach you more of man,
> Of moral evil and of good,
> Than all the ages can.
> Enough of science and of art,
> Close up those barren leaves.
> Come forth and bring with you a heart
> That watches and receives.

Walt Whitman, on the other hand, was an urbanite who from childhood lived in or near, and dearly loved, the great cities of the new world-- cities like New York and Washington D.C. Walt Whitman was certainly not a luddite. Whitman loved machines and machinery plays a major part in his poetry. And he loved progress. Whitman, unlike Wordsworth, could never get "enough of science and of art." He loved attending the great industrial expositions, the grand celebrations of human progress, that were held in the great cities of that time. Whitman even wrote a poem celebrating technological progress, "After All, Not to Create Only," later to be called "The Song of the Exposition," which he read at the opening of the American Institute of New York. Whitman, perhaps in contrast to Wordsworth, was in love with the modern world.

And yet Whitman shared Wordsworth's concerns: he knew that there was something lacking in the modern world. He knew that it was the poet's task, the prophet's task, the task of any valid contemporary religion, to put human beings back in living touch with Nature once again.

The impetus for Whitman's views about Nature probably can be found in his childhood jaunts on the Long Island shore where he learned to love the sea, where he identified with the plants and animals which were found there, and where he absorbed much of the imagery which, after being preserved in his prodigious memory, found expression in many of his poems. His father also knew the great Tom Paine, and Walt Whitman, while yet a young man, read Paine's great religious work, <u>The Age of Reason</u>. He learned from Paine, as he learned anew from reading Emerson's essay on "Nature" a few years later, that true revelation comes not from Bibles or creeds, but from Nature.

But his view of Nature was even more profoundly influenced, it seems to me, by his experience as an older man, after having a series of strokes which left him partially paralyzed—strokes which left him, as he said, "a half paralytic," or, as he put it in his autobiographical poem "Prayer of Columbus" a batter'd, wreck'd old man.

Whitman was living in Camden, New Jersey at the time, and became friends with a farm family, the Stafford family, who lived in the country not far from Camden. A creek ran through the Stafford Farm – "Timber Creek" – and along the creek was a woods and in that woods the poet found solace in Nature. Whitman communed with the creek and with the birds and with the trees, and in the process learned all of the species of flora and fauna to be found on Timber Creek. In the privacy of Timber Creek he would take off his clothes and let the sun minister to his body. He felt the healing power of Nature there on Timber Creek, and slowly regained much of his health and vigor. It was just about this time that he composed a little poem which he called "The Calming Thought of All."

> The calming thought of all
> That coursing on, whate'er men's speculations,
> Amid the changing schools, theologies, philosophies,
> Amid the bawling presentations new and old,
> The round earth's silent vital laws, facts, modes continue.

C

Walt Whitman loved the city, and he loved the machines and the other things that were the trappings of progress, and he saw himself as the poet of the modern. But he also loved

Nature, and saw himself as the prophet of Nature, of that which went "coursing on, whate'er men's speculations, Amid the changing schools, theologies, philosophies, Amid the bawling presentations new and old." Humanity changed over time, and the ideas people held about humanity were constantly being reformulated, but Nature was constant. It is Nature that is to be the enduring reality by which we are to know and understand human being. In Nature are found both the origins of human existence and the environment in which the human life is to be lived. The authentic prophet for the modern world, "The True Son of God" to use Whitman's phrase, has to place the human race back into the context of Nature once again.

"The sharp-hoov'd moose of the north, the cat on the house sill, the chickadee…," he wrote, in "Song of Myself," "I see in them, and in myself, the same old law." "The same old law" applies to both animals and human beings. We are both part of the one family of Nature. It is also in "Song of Myself," where Whitman sings, in a delightful and yet insightful, way about animals:

> I think I could turn and live with animals, they are
>   so placid and self-contained,
> I stand and look at them long and long.
>
> They do not sweat and whine about their condition,
> They do not lie awake in the dark and weep for their
>   sins,
> They do not make me sick discussing their duty to
>   God,
> Not one is dissatisfied, not one is demented with the
>   mania of owning things,
> Not one kneels to another, nor to his kind that lived
>   a thousand years ago,

> Not one is respectable or unhappy over the whole earth.
>
> So they show their relations to me and I accept them,
> They bring me tokens of myself, they evince them plainly in their possession.

"So they show their relations to me and I accept them," Whitman writes in the indicative words that conclude this section, "They bring me tokens of myself, they evince them plainly in their possession." If we are of the same family as the animals we can learn something from them if we open our eyes and become aware. The human animal often does spend a lot of time whining "about their condition;" does get caught up in "the mania of owning things;" does spend too much time "discussing their duty to God." If we accepted our place in Nature, Whitman is suggesting, we would be more comfortable, and confident, as human beings.

D

Walt Whitman shares with William Wordsworth an almost sacramental view of Nature, but in Whitman's prophetic vision there is also a profound love of humanity, the concrete humanity that lives in the modern, urban world. The function of "the true poet," the function of an adequate modern religion, Whitman feels, is to unite Nature and Humanity in one all encompassing vision. "The journey done, the journeyman come home," Whitman sings in "Proud Music of the Storm," indicating the hoped for conclusion of the prophetic task, "And Man and Art with Nature fused again."

This aspect of the prophetic vision of Walt Whitman is best expressed in a poem written near the end of his career. It is found in the collection called "Good-bye My Fancy."

> When the full grown poet came,
> Out spake pleased Nature (the round impassive globe, with all its shows of day and night) saying, He is mine;
> But out spake too the Soul of man, proud, jealous and unreconciled, Nay, he is mine alone;
> --Then the full-grown poet stood between the two, and took each by the hand;
> And to-day and ever so stands, as blender, uniter, tightly holding hands, which he will never release until he reconciles the two, and wholly and joyously blends them.

There is some powerful imagery in this little poem. There are those, like Wordsworth, who seemed to be saying that an adequate religion for the modern world has to be solely grounded in Nature. There are others, like some of the humanists of the time, who seemed to be saying that an adequate religion for the modern world had to be solely grounded in humanity, as if humanity transcended Nature. The prophet of religion for the modern world, Whitman is saying, must not accept either of these premises. The task of the "true poet" is to celebrate both Humanity and Nature, but more than that, to "wholly and joyously blend them."

This spirit – the spirit of uniting Humanity and Nature – is exhibited all through Leaves of Grass. A central premise of the prophetic vision of Walt Whitman is that of "blending" the human with the natural. It is not so much that he wanted to merge them in the sense that the two separate identities are lost, but to show an intrinsic relationship. The most appropriate metaphor to come to mind is that of marriage. One can almost see the metaphor of the wedding ceremony, it seems to me, with the "True Son of God" as the priest or minister, as a setting for Whitman's poem. In marriage the two people do not become less than they are—they remain two people—but a new union is formed, a vital living relationship. That new living relationship is frequently symbolized by the joining of hands. It is that type of relatedness which is central to Whitman's vision. Two principles, and two principals – Nature and Humanity – must be kept in mind, must be kept in "hand."

On the one hand is Nature, "the round impassive globe, with all its shows of day and night." What Whitman means by Nature, in these words, is the phenomenal world, the world of Nature, which we actually do experience, the world of trees and mountains and oceans and animals. That world has a claim on us –"He is Mine" –human beings are intrinsic aspects of the natural world.

On the other hand is humanity, "proud, jealous, unreconciled." In terms of Whitman's prophetic vision, though not separated from Nature, there is something special about the human. Humanity also has a claim on us – "He is Mine alone" – a claim that a religion for the modern world needs to appreciate. "O, wonder: How many goodly creatures are there here," exudes William Shakespeare, "How beauteous mankind is: O brave new world that has such people in it." Walt Whitman liked Shakespeare and if he was familiar with this passage he would have liked it as well. Shakespeare's words convey an important aspect of Whitman's prophetic vision.

Whitman may also have been familiar with the sermons of William Elery Channing, perhaps the greatest preacher of the first half of the 19th century. Whitman would at least have approved of these words from Channing's sermon titled "Likeness to God."

> I do and I must reverence human Nature. Neither the sneers of a worldly skeptic, nor the groans of a gloomy theology disturb my faith in its godlike powers and tendencies. I know how it is despised, how it has been oppressed.... I shut my eyes on none of its weaknesses and crimes....But I still turn to it with intense sympathy and strong hope...and I thank God that my own lot is bound up with that of the human race.

Walt Whitman has a profound "reverence" for human nature. Leaves of Grass is a constant witness to the fact of the poet's thankfulness that his "lot is bound up with that of the human race."

Whitman was in love with humanity. It is a theme touched on again and again in his book. "Everything, everything comes out of the people, everyday people," he told his friend Horace Traubel, "the people as you find them and leave them: people, people, just people." His religion for the modern world, though it had roots in the natural world, was centered on the human being and on that historical collection of human beings called humanity. Walt Whitman would have identified with the words of his great Italian contemporary, Giuseppe Mazzini:

> Thou cans't not, even if thou wouldst, separate thy life from that of humanity. Thou livest in it, by it and for it. Thy soul cannot separate itself from the elements amongst which it moves."

E

Religion in its fundamental sense, to use two phrases from Paul Tillich, deals with the "ground of being" and with matters of "ultimate concern." Religion asks questions about that which can be defined as being our "ground of being," about that in which we are most deeply and profoundly rooted, and about that to which we can give our "ultimate concern." The answers to such questions can provide us with some insight into that which is holy and that which is sacred.

Whitman's answers to such questions would be two-fold: Nature and Humanity. In the gospel according to Walt Whitman, Nature and Humanity are both holy. They are both sacred. An appropriate religion for the modern world, in terms of Whitman's prophetic vision, has to be "grounded" in an overarching natural view of the universe and grounded in an exalted appreciation of humanity. Both nature and humanity are, for him, matters of ultimate concern. The prophetic task is to wed them in a theology that rings true for the modern world. "Nature and Man shall be disjoin'd and diffused no more," he writes in "Passage to India," "The true son of God shall absolutely fuse them." When this happens then, perhaps, the human race can find an enduring sense of meaning once again.

Walt Whitman is both a humanist and a naturalist. His prophetic vision is one that embraces both humanism and naturalism. He is the prophet of a faith that seeks to celebrate the human being as having a rightful place in this world, the natural world, and of a humanity that enriches and sustains him or her.

CHAPTER XV
A VAST SIMILITUDE INTERLOCKS ALL

A vast similitude interlocks all,
All lives and deaths, all of the past, present, future,
This vast similitude spans them, and always has spann'd,
And shall forever span them and compactly hold and enclose them.
           "On The Beach at Night Alone"

A

In 1859 Charles Darwin published his monumental work on evolution, The Origin of Species. The ideas expressed by Darwin in that book evolved out of a journey he took, as a naturalist, on a ship called the Beagle. On that journey, which lasted from 1831 to 1836, and which spent time in the waters around South America and around the islands of the south Pacific, Darwin became convinced a process of evolution was at the very heart of nature. Because he knew that his conclusions would be controversial, he did not publish his great book for two decades, but once he did it was destined to alter and shape the way people look at themselves, the world, and the universe. "Charles Darwin saw a vision," Loren Eiseley wrote in his book, <u>Darwin's Century</u>, which was written to celebrate the centenary of Darwin's death:

> It was one of the most tremendous insights a living being ever had.... None of his forerunners had left such a message; none saw, in a similar manner, the whole vista of life with quite such sweeping vision.

What Darwin discovered on his voyage on the Beagle was that all living things are the result of a single process of evolution, that all living things, from one celled creatures to the so-called "higher animals," share common ancestors. "I can entertain no doubt, after the most deliberate study and dispassionate judgment of which I am capable," Darwin wrote:

> the view which most naturalists entertain, and which I formerly entertained – namely that each species are not immutable; but that those belonging to what are called the same genera are lineal descendants of some other and generally extinct species, in the same manner as the acknowledged varieties of any one species are the descendants of that species.

Darwin's discoveries, furthermore, were to drastically alter what he believed. This man, who had originally intended to become a clergyman, but who became a naturalist instead, eventually arrived at the place where he rejected Christianity, the dominant religious expression of his culture. "Disbelief crept over me at a very slow rate, but was at last complete," he wrote to a friend,

> The rate was so slow that I felt no distress, and have never since doubted even for a second that my

conclusions were correct. I can indeed hardly see how anyone ought to wish Christianity to be true; for if so, the plain language of the text seems to show that the men who do not believe, and this would include my father, brother, and almost all my best friends, will be everlastingly punished. And this is a damnable doctrine.

Damnable Doctrine! That was the response to his theory of evolution as soon as it became public and well known. It was denounced in churches and by eminent Christian clerics all over the English speaking world and it still is, to this day. Darwin himself could sense that something of the sacred, something of the holy, might be lost as the truth of evolution dawned on the soul. The great naturalist knew that the recognition of the truth of evolution would strike at the very root of Christianity; would strike at the religious underpinnings of the western world.

But if Darwin knew that evolution, as its deep meaning filtered into western consciousness, would undermine the tenets of established faith, he also knew that it contained a new foundation for awe and wonder which is at the heart of religion. If the insights Darwin gained on his voyage on the Beagle "took something away" from religion, they also "gave something back" to it:

> It is interesting to contemplate a tangled bank, clothed with many plants of many kinds, with birds singing in the bushes, with various insects flitting about, and with worms crawling through the damp earth and to reflect that these elaborately constructed forms, so different from each other, and dependent upon each other in so complex a manner, have all been produced by laws acting around us.

These laws, taken in the largest sense, being growth with reproduction; variability from the indirect and direct action of the conditions of life, and from use and disuse; a ratio of increase so high as to lead to a struggle for life, and as a consequence to natural selection, entailing divergence of character and the extinction of less-improved forms. Thus, from the war of nature, from famine and death, the most exalted object which we are capable of conceiving, namely, the production of the higher animals, directly follows. There is grandeur in this view of life,...that, whilst this planet has gone cycling on according to the fixed laws of gravity, from so simple a beginning endless forms most wonderful and most beautiful have been, and are, being evolved.

B

"There is grandeur in this view of life." So thought Charles Darwin in England; and so thought Walt Whitman in America. I do not know when Whitman first learned of Darwin's ideas, but that he dealt with the subject is clear from a brief essay he wrote late in his life. The theory of evolution "has so much in it, and is so needed as a counterpoint to yet widely prevailing and unspeakably tenacious, enfeebling superstitions," he wrote in "Notes Left Over,"

> that the world of erudition, both moral and spiritual, cannot but be eventually better'd and broadened in it speculations, from the advent of Darwinism.

I expect, however, that Whitman's own ideas of evolution were influenced by Darwin, or at least by evolutionary theory, at a much earlier date. His reference to evolutionary ideas in "Song of Myself," in fact, predate the publication of Darwin's Origin of Species. It would appear that Whitman, as one who tended to keep up with the times, must have been familiar with the controversy over evolution that began before Darwin and that the publication of The Origin of Species would fuel. After all, the idea of evolution was not new. It was as old as the ancient world. Certainly Whitman had read the Roman poet and philosopher, Lucretius, 4th century B.C.E., who outlined, in powerful poetic form, the outlines of evolution, who spoke of the relatedness of all things, and then concluded,

> How true remains,
> How merited is that adopted name
> Of earth – "the mother!" – since from out of the earth
> All are begotten. And even now arise
> From out the loams how many living things –
> Concreted by the rains and heat of the sun.

Whatever may have been its particular sources, the theme of evolution, both in its general terms and its biological meaning, are found throughout Leaves of Grass. One can say without reservation that Whitman was an evolutionist, that he saw the shape of his own life, and the lives of others as the product of evolutionary change, and that he saw the world as being in constant evolutionary change. "We have thus far exhausted trillions of winters and summers," he says in "Song of Myself," "There are trillions ahead, and trillions ahead of them." Over these "trillions" and "trillions" of summers and winters the earth, nature, and life has been unfolding. And, for Whitman, there is a powerful sense of marvel and awe that out of this unfolding, human beings, like himself, and like you and me, have evolved. In "Song of Myself" he sings a hymn to evolution in words that are as scientific accurate as they are poetically beautiful.

>Long I was hugg'd close – long and long,

>Immense have been the preparations for me
>Before I was born out of my mother generations guided me,
>My embryo has never been torpid, nothing could overlay it.

>For it the nebula cohered to an orb,
>The long strata piled to rest it on,
>Vast vegetables gave it sustenance,
>Monstrous sauroids transported it in their mouths and deposited it with care.

>All forces have been steadily employ'd to complete and delight me,
>Now on this spot I stand with my robust soul.

All of us, through the workings of nature, are the result of a continuous process that goes back to the earliest beginnings of life on this planet. Whitman knew instinctively what nineteenth century and twentieth century science was to verify.

C

The science of the 19th century verified that all life on this planet is the product of a single evolutionary process. Somehow matter sparked to life in some primordial waters, and out of that spark, and over eons of time, all of the living forms that do, or have, made their homes on planet

Earth have come. The answer is "Yes" to the question posed by Guy de Maupassant,

> For was it not in stagnant and muddy waters, amid the heavy humidity of moist land under the heat of the sun, that the first germ of life pulsated and expanded to the day?

The science of the twentieth century has added to that legacy, however, and verified that not only life on this planet, but all of the animate and inanimate things in the entire universe are part of a single unfolding evolutionary process. In the nineteenth century we learned that our beginnings were three or four billions of years back in time, back to those first origins of life. In the twentieth century we have learned that we were many more billions of years in the making. We learned that the very materials that form our bodies were formed in the center of dying stars. We learned that the process of evolution was, and is, continuous through all time, that this universe of nature in which we live is now revealed as a single process of evolution.

This story is a new Genesis, a new understanding of human beginnings and origins. In terms of that new Genesis, we can trace our own origins back to the moment of creation. The moment of creation! That's fourteen or fifteen billion years ago by the best and most usual accounts. Fourteen or fifteen billion years ago and a grand explosion! – A grand explosion beyond human comprehension, called "The Big Bang" – a grand explosion that set in motion and generated a sequence of events that tells us that everything – from stars to animals, from trees to people, from stones to galaxies – are part of a single evolutionary process.

"The philosophy that we are the products of cosmic evolution is not a new one," notes astrophysicist Eric Chaisson, at the time a faculty member at Harvard,

> It may be as old as that first homo sapiens who contemplated existence. But well into the last quarter of the twentieth century we can begin to identify conceptually and to test experimentally some of the subtle astrophysical and biological processes that enable us to recognize the cosmos as the ground and origin of our existence. It is very much an interdisciplinary approach, interweaving knowledge from virtually every subject a university can offer. It is a warmer and friendlier scenario now, many parts of which recently have become substantiated by experimental science. We are not independent entities, alien to earth. Earth in turn is not adrift in a vacuum unrelated to the cosmos. The cosmos itself is no longer cold and hostile because it is our universe. It brought us forth, and it maintains our being. We are, in the very literal sense of the word, children of the universe.

D

We are, quite literally, children of the universe! "Are not the mountains, waves and skies a part of me and of my soul and I of them," asked Lord Byron, a generation before Whitman's time. The American poet would have nodded in agreement. "Shall I not have intelligence with the earth?" asks his great contemporary Henry David Thoreau, "Am I not partly leaves and vegetable mould myself?" Whitman would have responded in the affirmative. When poets and scientists today remind us that our blood is like salt water, that we are made of stardust, that life became possible only because of intercourse between the sun and the earth, they have a kindred spirit in Walt Whitman.

It was of the essence of Whitman's conviction, as a poet, and as a prophet, that all things are interrelated. Human beings, animals, plants, stars and the whole cosmos, for Walt Whitman, are of one family. One of Whitman's words for this is "similitude." The <u>American Heritage Dictionary</u> defines "similitude" as "something closely resembling another; a counterpart; double." The entire universe, and all of time, are part of this vast "similitude," part of a vast unfolding process. The human being – Whitman's "I" – is a part of that unfolding. When one sees that unfolding as the ultimate reality, and the feeling of self as a part of it, then one can feel, as Whitman felt, that long before birth, and long after death, we exist. All of us are continuing fragments of that whole. Whitman unfolds this whole grand scheme in a poem called "On the Beach Alone At Night."

> On the beach at night alone,
> As the old mother sways her to and fro singing her husky song,
>
> As I watch the bright stars shining, I think a thought of the clef of the universes and the future.
>
> A vast similitude interlocks all,
> All spheres, grown, ungrown, small, large, suns, moons, planets,
> All distances of place however wide,
> All distances of time, all inanimate forms, all souls,
> All living bodies though they be ever so different, or in different worlds,
> All gaseous, watery, vegetable, mineral processes, the fishes, the brutes,

> All nations, colors, barbarisms, civilizations, languages,
> All identities that have existed or may exist on this globe, or any globe,
> All lives and deaths, all of the past, present, future,
> This vast similitude spans them, and always has span'd,
> And shall forever span them and compactly hold and enclose them.

It is this perspective that provides an understanding of the core of Whitman's mysticism. It is not a mysticism grounded in the supernatural. It is a mysticism grounded in the very physical and material universe that the science of the modern world is unfolding. John Addington Symonds, in his powerful reflection on Whitman, published the year after Whitman's death, beautifully captures this spirit:

> There is no finality in any creed, nor can there be, because man's place in the universe is but a speck of cloud in an illimitable sky, a fragment of straw afloat upon a boundless ocean. This does not prevent what Whitman calls religion – that is to say, a sturdy confidence in the security of the whole scheme of things, a sense of universal life and of our indestructible participation in the same—from being for him the most important of all human facts and qualities.
>
> The secret of Whitman, his inner wisdom, consists in attaining an attitude of confidence, a sense of security, by depending on the great thought of the universe, to which all things including our particular selves are attached by an indubitable link of vital participation. This religion corresponds exactly to

the scientific principle of the modern age; to the evolutionary hypothesis with its display of an immense unfolding organism, to the correlation of forces and the conservation of energy, which forbid the doubt of any atom wasted, any part mismade or unaccounted for eventually.

Sustained by this conception that nothing can be ultimately lost, or doomed to pain, or annihilated, in the universal frame, Whitman feels strong enough to cry:

> My foot is tenoned and mortised in granite
> I laugh at what you call dissolution,
> And I know the amplitude of time.

Still I may point out that it is the only type of faith which agrees with the conclusions and determinations of science. To bear the yoke of universal law is the plain destiny of human beings. If we could learn to bear that yoke with gladness, to thrill with vibrant fibers to the pulses of the infinite machine we constitute…if, I say, we could feel pride and joy in our participation of the cosmic life, then we might stand where Whitman stood with "feet tenoned and mortised in granite."

E

Walt Whitman's great contemporary, Alfred Lord Tennyson, mused over a "flower in a crannied wall," and thought that if he could discover what that flower was, he "should know what God and man is." Whitman, no more than Tennyson, really knows "what God and man is," but Whitman does know that the answer, for the modern world, is to be found in an acceptance of an intrinsic relatedness with all that is. One must approach that vast similitude with awe and wonder, and with love. One must place one's confidence in that vast similitude, and know that it is the source of happiness and meaning. Students of Whitman can not be certain that Whitman had an extensive knowledge of the sacred scriptures of India, but his thoughts reflect one of the great dialogues found in the <u>Upanishads.</u> It is a dialogue between a father and his son. The father speaks first: "Fetch me thence a fruit of the banyan tree." The son responds: "Here is one, sir." And the dialog continues:

"Break it."
"It is broken, Sir."
"What do you see there?"
"These seeds, almost infinitesimal."
"Break one of them."
"It is broken, Sir."
"What do you see there?"
"Not anything, Sir."

The father said, "My son, that subtle essence which you do not perceive there, of that very essence this great banyan tree exists. Believe it, my son. That which is the subtle essence, in all that exists has itself. It is the True. It is the Self, and thou, O Svetaketu, art it.

"I say the whole earth, and all the stars in the sky, are for religion's sake," Whitman wrote in the preface to the first edition of <u>Leaves of Grass</u>. It is a conviction that remained with him all of his life. The primary imperative of religion for the modern world is to put human beings back in touch with that earth and with that sky, to put people back in touch with the universe as it has been unfolding in our time.

"It is a question of relationship," wrote D. H. Lawrence in the twentieth century, again in words that Whitman would support,

> We must get back into relation, vivid and nourishing relation to the cosmos and the universe: for the truth is we are perishing for lack of fulfillment of our greater needs, we are cut off from the great sources of our inward nourishment and renewal, sources which flow eternally in the universe. Vitally, the human race is dying. It is like a great uprooted tree, with its roots in the air. We must plant ourselves again in the universe."

The gospel of Walt Whitman "plants" human beings "again in the Universe." "The known universe has one complete lover and that is the greatest of poets," Whitman says in his preface to the first edition of Leaves of Grass. The authentic prophet of religion for the modern world, he is saying, must have a love affair with the physical universe and with the interrelatedness of all things which that universe engenders. His vision of inter-relatedness, which begins with the embodied self and intimate human relationships, expands through communal and social relationships to embrace the whole human family, and then continues to expand through relationships that involve life on this planet and, ultimately, the cosmic relatedness of all things. It is out of this cosmic relatedness that human meaning and human love emerges. There are no more beautiful words to describe this, in our day, than those of Robert Weston:

Out of the stars in their flight, out of the dust of
 eternity, here have we come,
Stardust and sunlight, mingling through time and
 through space.
Out of the stars have we come, up from time;
Out of the stars have we come.
Time out of time before time in the vastness of
 space, earth spun to orbit the sun,
Earth with the thunder of mountains newborn, the
 boiling of seas,
Earth warmed by sun, lit by sunlight: this is our
 home;
Out of the stars have we come.
Mystery hidden in mystery, back through all time;
Mystery rising from rocks in the storm and the sea.
Out of the stars, rising from rocks and the sea,
Kindled by sunlight on earth, arose life.
Ponder this thing in your heart; ponder with awe:
Out of the sea to the land, out of the shallows came
 ferns.
Out of the sea to the land, up from darkness to light,
Rising to walk and to fly, out of the sea trembled
 life.
Ponder this thing in your heart, life up from the sea;
Eyes to behold, throats to sing, mates to love.
Life from the sea, warmed by sun, washed by rain,
Life from within, giving birth rose too love.
This is the wonder of time; this is the marvel of
 space;
Out of the stars swung the earth; life upon earth rose
 to love.
This is the marvel of man, rising to see and to
 know;
Out of you heart, cry wonder: sing that we live.

CHAPTER XVI
DEATH IS THE HARVEST

As I watched the ploughman ploughing,
Or the sower sowing in the fields, or the harvester harvesting,
I saw there too, O life and death, your analogies;
(Life, life is the tillage, and death is the harvest according.)
                      "Whispers of Heavenly Death"

A

After four years of suffering and severe disability, Walt Whitman died—"with apologies for the length of his dying" –in Camden, New Jersey, on March 26, 1892. By this time the author of <u>Leaves of Grass</u> had received considerable fame and there were major stories, about his life and death, in all of the major newspapers of America and many in Europe as well.

Walt Whitman was buried four days later on a lot in Harleigh Cemetery which the city of Camden had given to him. In the year prior to his death he had arranged for a "plain massive stone temple" of "unpolished Quincy granite" to be constructed on that site for his final resting place. Whitman himself designed the tomb which was based on William Blake's etching, "Death's Door." The tomb has only the words "Walt Whitman" engraved on it, but later, as he had planned, the bodies of his parents, his sister Hannah, his brothers, George and Eddy, along with George's wife and their infant son were also entombed there.

When Walt Whitman was having his tomb constructed, most of his friends objected, thinking the whole thing was "foolishness." They insisted that he was spending too much money—money he did not have. But Whitman persisted. All of his life he had insisted of <u>Leaves of Grass</u>, "Comarado, this is no book, who touches this touches a man," and he needed a place, a visible place, a shrine, where his prophetic vision might be permanently marked. If <u>Leaves of Grass</u> survived across the generations, he felt, then his tomb would become a kind of shrine.

His funeral was a great public event in Camden, New Jersey which, by this time, had claimed Walt Whitman as its own native son. Thousands of people marched through his home on Mickle Street to view his body, and more thousands followed the procession to Harleigh Cemetery. It was an unusual funeral service—especially for his time. In addition to the Bible, there were readings from Confucius, Gautama, Plato, the Koran, and <u>Leaves of Grass</u>. One of the most noted public speakers of the time, Colonel Robert Ingersol, "the Great Agnostic," gave the funeral address. Ingersol's funeral address, in which he referred to Whitman as "the most eminent citizen of this republic," is, in itself, a very stirring piece of literature. The twentieth century poet, Carl Sandburg, said, "Ingersol on Whitman is a precious thing, a treasure." Here are several of the jewels in that "treasure."

MY FRIENDS: Again we, in the mystery of Life, are brought face to face with the mystery of Death. A great man, a great American, the most eminent citizen of this republic, lies dead before us, and we have met to pay a tribute to his greatness and his worth.

One of the greatest lines in our literature is his, and the line is great enough to do honor to the greatest genius that has ever lived. He said, speaking of an outcast: "Not till the sun excludes you do I exclude you."

He was the poet of Life. It was a joy simply to breathe. He loved the clouds; he enjoyed the breath of morning, the twilight, the wind, the winding streams. He loved to look at the sea when the waves burst into the whitecaps of joy.

He was the poet of Love. He was not ashamed of that divine passion that has built every home in the world; that divine passion that has painted every picture and given us every real work of art....

He was the poet of the natural, and taught men not to be ashamed of that which is natural. He was not only the poet of democracy, not only the poet of the great Republic, but he was the poet of the human race.

He wrote a liturgy for mankind; he wrote a great and splendid psalm of life, and he gave to us the gospel of humanity –the greatest gospel that can be preached.

Today we give back to Mother Nature, to her clasp and kiss, one of the bravest sweetest souls that ever lived in human clay.

Charitable as the air and generous as Nature, he was negligent of all except to do and say what he believed he should do and should say.

And I today thank him, not only for you but for myself, for all the brave words he has uttered. I thank him for the great and splendid words he has said in favor of liberty, in favor of man and woman, in favor of motherhood, in favor of fathers, in favor of children, and I thank him for the brave words that he has said of death.

He has lived, he has died, and death is less terrible than it was before. Thousands and millions will walk down into the "dark valley of the shadow" holding Walt Whitman by the hand. Long after we are dead the brave words he has spoken will sound like trumpets to the dying.

And so I lay this little wreath upon this great man's tomb. I loved him living, and I love him still.

B

"I thank him for the brave words that he has said of death," said Ingersol, "He has lived, he has died, and death is less terrible than it was before." Walt Whitman had many words to say about death—brave and otherwise—and his words have been helpful and comforting to many people as they have faced their own deaths and the deaths of those they love.

Death is one of the major themes of Leaves of Grass. With the possible exception of the self, there are more lines committed to this theme, in his book, than to any other. The importance of this theme to the poet is evidenced by the fact, as Whitman stated in the 1876 edition of Leaves of Grass, that he had intended to write a companion volume to Leaves entirely on the subject of death. He was never able to accomplish this task, but the subject is found throughout his work. Some of his greatest poems—like his masterpiece, "When Lilacs Last in Dooryards Bloom'd"— and many other less important poems as well, deal with death.

Whitman deals with death, in many cases by referring to his own inevitable death. Many years before his death, for example, he wrote his own epitaph:

> Dear Friend whoever you are take this kiss,
> I give it especially to you, do not forget me,
> I feel like one who has done work for the day to retire awhile,
>   …So Long! I love you,
> I depart from materials. I am as one disembodied, triumphant, dead.

There is a great deal of such acceptance of death in Leaves of Grass. "I know I am deathless," he says in "Song of Myself," and adds in his "Song of Joys," "For not life's joys alone I sing, repeating – the joy of death!"

There is not only acceptance but also celebration of death in Leaves of Grass, such as in his magnificent elegy on the death of Abraham Lincoln, "When Lilacs Last in Door Yard Bloom'd,"

> Come lovely and soothing death,
> Undulate round the world, serenely arriving, arriving,
> In the day, in the night, to all, to each,
> Sooner or later delicate death.

Or, even more emphatically in his "Passage to India," where he is urging the reader to make passage to "more than India," to death itself,

> Sail forth – steer for the deep waters only,
> Reckless O soul, exploring, I with thee, and thou with me,
> For we are bound where mariner has not yet dared to go,
> And we will risk the ship, ourselves and all.
>
> O my brave soul!
> O farther farther sail!
> O darling joy, but safe! Are they not all the seas of God?
> O farther, farther, farther sail!

Just as there are many references to death in Leaves of Grass, there is also a great deal of attention paid to its companion subject, immortality. The poet was a fervent believer in immortality. "When I say immortality I say identity," he told his friend Horace Traubel, "The survival of the personal soul – your survival, my survival."

Whitman believed that everything in the universe had an eternal soul, an idea that finds expression throughout his work. "If maggots and rats ended us, then alarum!" he writes in "To Think of Time," "for we are betrayed." "Of your real body and any man or woman's real body," he adds in "Starting from Paumonak," "Item for item it will elude the hands of the corpse-cleaners and pass to fitting spheres." And in "Song of Myself:"

> What do you think has become of the young and old men?
>
> And what do you think has become of the women and the children?
>
> They are alive and well somewhere,
> The smallest sprout shows there is really no death,
> And if ever there was it led forward life, and does not wait at the end to arrest it,
> And ceas'd the moment life appeare'd.
>
> All goes onward and outward, nothing collapses,
> And to die is different from what any one supposed, and luckier.
>
> Has any one supposed it lucky to be born?
> I hasten to inform him or her it is just as lucky to die, and I know it.
> ...
>
> I am the mate and companion of people, all just as immortal and fathomless as myself,
> (They do not know how immortal, but I know.)

Walt Whitman had a lot to say about death and immortality, but one should not imagine that he had a comprehensive and cohesive theory about the subject. Death was for him, as it must be for all people, enshrouded in mystery. In "Song of Myself" he says of "being" that it is "the puzzle of puzzles." He constantly sees death as a great "mystery" and although he believes in immortality he sometimes has his doubts. Those doubts are well expressed in "Thought," one of the poems in "Whispers of Heavenly Death." In the poem he is musing on a great ship that is wrecked and sinking with women on the deck about to be drowned. The poem ends with these words:

> Sinking there while the passionate wet flows on –
>   and I now pondering
> Are these women indeed gone?
> Are souls drown'd and destroy'd so?
> Is only matter triumphant?

"Is only matter triumphant?" In times of doubt the poet is not sure, but faith usually brings him back to the intuition that whatever else may be true about death, death must be a good. "Pleasantly and well-suited, wither I walk I cannot define, but I know it is good," he sings in "To Think of Time," "The whole universe indicates that it is good, the past and the present indicate that it is good." Not sure what it is that death might be, and aware of how little human beings can really know of what lies beyond the grave, Walt Whitman, nevertheless, approaches it with confidence.

> I do not know what is untried and afterward,
> But I know it will in its turn prove sufficient, and
>   cannot fail.

Whitman's views of death and immortality—however powerfully they may be expressed in his poetry—seem at times inconsistent with the naturalistic, humanistic, and materialistic elements characteristic of his prophetic vision.

"The immortal poets have done their work and pass'd to other spheres," Whitman sings in "By Blue Ontario's

Shores," "A work remains, the work of surpassing all that they have done." Walt Whitman understands his own prophetic mission as undertaking that "work" by recognizing that the old religions are obsolete, and by articulating new ways of understanding the universe which are more compatible with modern thought.

His views of death often seem to reiterate the ideas of the old religions, however, and not to move on to a new understanding, consistent with the way moderns, in an age of science, can understand the universe. Whitman and Robert Ingersol, who gave the eulogy at Whitman's funeral service, argued at times about this very point.

But not all of Whitman's views of death harken back to the old faiths. Although he often sees death as a supreme good, he also sees life as a supreme good and death as a characteristic of life. Life is good even if death is the end. There are times when it seems that the poet might have agreed with his friend Robert Ingersol:

> It may be that death gives all there is of worth to life. If those we press and strain within our arms could never die, perhaps that love would wither from the earth. Maybe this common fate treads from out the paths between our hearts the weeds of selfishness and hate. And I had rather live and love where death is king, than have eternal life where love is not.

Whitman could also imagine a world where death is absolute and yet worth the price it exacts for life. This view, along with some of Whitman's doubts, find expression in a lovely poem from "Calamus" which is called "Of the Terrible Doubts of Appearances:"

Of the terrible doubts of appearances,
Of the uncertainty after all that we may be deluded,
That may-be reliance and hopes are speculations after all,
That may-be identity beyond the grave is a beautiful fable only,
May-be the things I perceive, the animals, plants, men, hills, shining and flowing waters,
The skies of day and night, colors, densities, forms, may-be these are (as doubtless they are) only apparitions, and the real something has yet to be known,
(How often they dart out of themselves as if to confound and mock me!
How often I think neither I know, nor any man knows, aught of them,)
May-be seeming to me what they are (as doubtless they indeed might seem) as from my present point of view, and might prove (as of course they would) nought of what they appear or naught anyhow, from entirely changed points of view;
To me these and the like of these are curiously answer'd by my lovers, my dear friends,
When he whom I love travels with me or sits a long while holding me by the hand,
When the subtle air, the impalpable, the sense that words and reason hold not, surround us and pervade us,
Then I am charged with untold and untellable wisdom, I am silent, I require nothing further,
I cannot answer the question of appearances or that of identity beyond the grave,
But I walk or sit indifferent, I am satisfied,
He ahold of my hand has completely satisfied me.

Whitman recognizes in this poem that he, and no other mortal as well, can answer the question of "identity beyond the grave," but one can affirm that, even when faced with the inevitability of death, life is precious. It is precious because, in life, we can experience the world. It is precious because, in life, we can experience love.

D

It is when Whitman sees death in the context of the processes of Nature, however, that the poet most fulfills the expectations of the other aspects of his prophetic vision. Death then becomes part of the cycles of the universe, of the ebb and flow of time, of the changes of existence which find their analog in the seasons of the year. We come out of the earth, live our lives and return to the earth again. The earth is mother. The earth is both our womb and our tomb.

"I bequeath myself to the dirt to grow from the grass I love," Whitman sings in some very indicative words found in "Song of Myself," "If you want me again look for me under your boot-soles." Grass is for Whitman—as the title of his book suggests—the universal symbol. Grass is found everywhere in the world. To die is to return to the grass. In death we do not cease to be: our elements become part of the continuing, and universal, processes of nature.

The best example of this aspect of Whitman's view of death is found in his poem "This Compost" which is located in the collection of poems called "Autumn Rivulets." "This Compost," which originally had the title "Poem at the Wonder of the Resurrection of Wheat," was first published in 1856, shortly after the death of Whitman's father but was constantly revised throughout the poet's lifetime. The poem begins:

Something startles me where I thought I was safest,
I withdraw from the still woods I loved,
I will not go now to the pastures to walk,
I will not strip the clothes from my body to meet my
　　lover the sea
I will not touch my flesh to the earth as to other
　　flesh to renew me.
O how can it be that the ground itself does not
　　sicken?
How can you be alive you growths of spring?
How can you furnish health you blood of herbs,
　　roots, orchards, grain?
Are they not continually putting distemper'd
　　corpses within you?
Is not every continent work'd over and over with
　　sour dead?

"Behold this compost!" writes Whitman. "Behold it well!" It would seem that every part of the earth of the world has once "form'd part of a sick person." "Drunkards and gluttons" of many generations have been placed in the earth. "Foul liquid and meat" has been dumped in the earth. The poet is afraid that if he plows the earth or digs in it with a spade, that he shall surely expose "some of the foul meat."

"Yet behold," he goes on:

　　　　The grass of spring covers the prairies,
　　　　The bean bursts noiselessly through the
　　　　　　mound in the garden,
　　　　The delicate spear of the onion pierces
　　　　　　upward,
　　　　The apple-buds cluster together on the
　　　　　　apple-branches,

> The resurrection of the wheat appears with paled visage out of its graves,
> The tinge awakens over the willow-tree and the mulberry-tree,
> The he-birds carol mornings and evening while the she-birds sit on their nests,
> The young of poultry break through the hatch'd eggs,
> The new-born of animals appear, the calf is dropt from the cow, the colt from the mare,
> Out of its little hill faithfully rise the potato's dark green leaves,
> Out of its hill rises the yellow maize-stalk, the lilacs bloom in the dooryards,
> The summer growth is innocent and disdainful above all those strata of sour dead.

"What chemistry!" the poet exudes, "That the winds are really not infectious," that it is safe to let the sea "lick my naked body all over with its tongues," that I will not be endangered "with the fevers that have deposited themselves in it," that "all is clean forever and forever." And then the poet concludes:

> Now I am terrified at the Earth, it is that calm and patient,
> It grows such sweet things out of such corruptions,
> It turns harmless and stainless on its axis, with such endless successions of diseas'd corpses,
> It distills such exquisite winds out of such infused fetor,
> It renews with such unwitting looks its prodigal, annual, sumptuous crops,

> It gives such divine materials to men, and accepts such leavings from them at last.

There are some who, upon reading this poem, fail to see the irony, and even the humor, in it. Whitman was always surprised by those who felt that he had no sense of humor. Some imagine that he was actually expressing the horror with which he begins the poem and the terror with which he concludes it. But it seems more appropriate to understand that Whitman was feigning horror, and using this as a poetic device to make a point. Death is part of a natural composting project, part of a cosmic recycling effort.

"Every part of nature teaches that the passing away of one life is the making of room for another," wrote Henry David Thoreau, "The oak dies down to the ground, leaving within its rind a virgin mould, which will impart a vigorous life to an infant forest. So our human life but dies down to its root, and still puts forth its green blade to eternity." It is something similar to this which Whitman is expressing in "This Compost." Life and death are part of a natural cycle in which new life is ever emerging. Human life "dies down to its root" and become a part of the life of the earth which has always brought the poet great joy and which, in Whitman's words, "is clean for ever and ever."

E

Just as there is a strong naturalistic element in Whitman's view of death, there is a strong humanistic element in his view of immortality. Just as the poet says that you should look for him "under your boot-soles" when he is dead, Whitman says that you should look for him in his book—in <u>Leaves of Grass</u> – after he is dead. His book is, for Whitman, one of the important artifacts of his life. The human being, even after death, can leave a legacy for those who follow after. The most powerful and personal expression of this in Leaves of Grass is found in "Crossing Brooklyn Ferry." In this poem the poet, on the ferry, is musing on the generations after him who will also make the crossing. "And you that shall cross from shore to shore years hence are more to me and more in my meditations, than you might suppose," the poet writes, "I am with you, men and women of a generation, or ever so many generations, hence. Just as you feel when you look on the river and sky, so I felt."

How is the poet, long dead, "with" those who now experience life? One of the ways is through their reading of his book. "Consider, you who peruse me," Whitman writes, "Whether I may not in unknown ways be looking upon you." The poet may be dead, but he is alive in the interactions between the dead poet and the living reader. The dead may be buried in the ground but they live in the artifacts that they leave behind. In known ways they live in the memories that are preserved just as Whitman himself surely lives in the hearts of those who know Leaves of Grass. In unknown ways they live on in the effects they have on the lives of all who follow, as they live on in me.

"Life is the tillage," Whitman sings in "Whispers of Heavenly Death," "and Death is the harvest, according." Death is the harvest of our lives. In life we are in the process of becoming, we are in the process of growing. Death defines, for all eternity, who we were. In death, we go back into the eternal processes of nature and of human existence. In death, we who were once only a part, as it were, return to the whole.

CHAPTER XVII
THE ROAD IS BEFORE US

Afoot and light-hearted I take to the open road,
Healthy, free the world before me,
The long brown path before me leading wherever I choose.

Henceforth I ask not good-fortune, I myself am good-fortune,
Henceforth I whimper no more, postpone no more, need nothing,
Done with indoor complaints, libraries, querulous criticisms,
Strong and content I travel the open road.
            "Song of the Open Road"

A

In February of 1848, at the age of twenty-nine, seven years before he published the first edition of Leaves of Grass, Walt Whitman was out of work. A year or so earlier he had been editor of the Brooklyn Eagle, but he had been fired from that job, "the best sit of his life," because of his "barnburner" objections to the extension of slavery in the western territories. Then, in one of those happenstance experiences which were to change his life, Whitman ran into J. E. McClure during the intermission at the Broadway

Theater. McClure was starting a daily newspaper in New Orleans, the <u>Daily Crescent</u>, and needed a chief editor. Over drinks during that intermission, McClure offered the job to Whitman and provided him with a two hundred dollar cash advance for travel expense. Within forty-eight hours, Walt Whitman, along with his younger brother, Jeff, was on his way to Louisiana.

In that time, the period before the Civil War, a journey to New Orleans was rather difficult and took two weeks to complete. Whitman had to take the train from New York to Cumberland, the end of the rail line. From Cumberland he had to take a stagecoach to Wheeling. At Wheeling, on the Ohio River, he boarded the steam packet St. Cloud which was bound for New Orleans from Pittsburgh. He was twelve days along the way.

Walt Whitman remained in New Orleans for only three months. For some reason he had to resign his position with the <u>Crescent</u> and set about to return to his home in Brooklyn. On his return journey he went up the Mississippi to Saint Louis, traveled on through Chicago and into Milwaukee. He was really impressed with Wisconsin. "It seems to me if we should ever remove from Long Island," he wrote in his notebook, "Wisconsin would be the proper place to come to." After leaving Milwaukee he went north to Mackinaw, then south to Detroit, and on to Buffalo in New York. From Buffalo he took an excursion to Niagara Falls, where he "went under the falls – saw the whirlpool and all the other sights." After visiting the falls he went on to Albany and down the Hudson River to New York.

Whitman's trip to the then west – through states such as Ohio, Illinois, Missouri, Wisconsin, and Michigan –provide the geographical setting for his book, <u>Leaves of Grass</u>, which was to emerge seven years later. "Out of such experiences," the poet said, "came the physiology of Leaves of Grass."

Many years later – when Whitman was sixty years old and, as he said, a "half-paralytic," Whitman made another journey, a journey he had dreamed about all of his life. In 1879 Colonel John W. Forney, publisher of the Philadelphia Press and the Old Settlers of Kansas Committee invited him to be the guest of honor at the Kansas Quarter Centennial Exposition to be held in Lawrence, Kansas. On that journey, which was by this time all by rail, he crossed Missouri which he thought to be a most impressive state and he loved the prairies of Kansas. After the exposition he was able to go on to Denver and to travel on into the Rocky Mountains which he had loved in his heart but was to see for the fist time. Of all the places he visited there was one place in Colorado that particularly stood out in his mind. That place was Platte Canyon. On viewing the canyon, Walt Whitman declared, "I have found the law of my own poems."

The great poet was to make one more major trip. His friend Dr. Richard Maurice Bucke, the director of an "insane asylum" in London, Ontario, had frequently urged him to come and visit him in Canada. In 1880, a few months after his return from his great "western jaunt," Whitman accepted this invitation and set out for Canada. Once again he stopped to see the great falls at Niagara. With Dr. Bucke he made a long, leisurely cruise down the St. Lawrence River and visited the great French Canadian city of Montreal. All in all, he remained in Canada for three months before returning to his home which was, at this time, in Camden, New Jersey.

Walt Whitman was a traveler. It was in his blood. As a boy he wandered all around Long Island absorbing all that he could see and find. As a man he traveled to New Orleans and to Colorado and to Canada. When he could not actually travel, he traveled the world in his mind and in his imagination. He always responded to the spirit that is so well expressed in Rudyard Kipling's "The Explorer."

> "There's no sense in going further – it's the edge of cultivation,"
> So they said, and I believed it – broke my land and sowed my crop—
> Built my barns and strung my fences in the little border station
> Tucked away below the foothills where the trails run out and stop.
>
> Till a voice, as bad as conscience, rang interminable changes
> On one everlasting whisper day and night repeated - - so:
> "Something hidden. Go and find it. Go and look behind the ranges –
> Something lost behind the ranges. Lost and waiting for you. Go!"

B

Walt Whitman, in his imagination and in his life, was a traveler, and, as a poet, he saw all of life and all of human experience as a journey. The journey motif is found all through Leaves of Grass, and is intimately connected to his prophetic vision. The "journey" image is found in the first long poem in the final edition of Leaves of Grass, following some brief "Inscriptions." It is titled "Starting from Paumanok." "Starting from fish-shaped Paumanok where I was born," he begins, "After roaming many lands, lover of populous pavements,"

> Far from the clank of crowds intervals passing rapt and happy,
> Aware of the fresh free giver the flowing Missouri, aware of mighty Niagara,
> Aware of the buffalo herds grazing the plains, the hirsute and strong-breasted bull,
> Of earth, rocks, fifth-month flowers experienced, stars, rain, snow, my amaze,
> Having studied the mocking-bird's tones and the flight of the mountain hawk,
> And heard at dawn the unrivall'd one, the hermit thrush from the swamp-cedars,
> Solitary, singing in the West, I strike up for a New World.

The symbolism is very important here. Paumanok is the Native American name for Long Island—which Whitman says is "fish-shaped" – the place of the poet's birth and boyhood. As a boy, Walt Whitman explored "Paumanok," its fields and shores, and gathered information about the geography of that world. As a man he moved out, "starting from Paumanok" to embrace larger and larger portions of the geography of the new world. But not geography only. He moved out to embrace the people and the ideas of the new world. But not the new world only, the people and ideas of the whole world. And not the present world only, but the world of the past as well. "Starting from Paumanok" Walt Whitman could go back in time to explore how people of the past, who at core are always very much like us, experienced their world in a different way.

We all start from Paumanok. In our separate journeys we all start from the place of our birth and move out to experience more and more of the world. In our journeys through life we start from the time of our birth and can, through books, imagination, and experience move beyond our time, to cultures and ideas that come from other parts of the world or from other times in human history.

That is true of religion as well. We are born into a culture. We are born into a prevailing religion that is characteristic of our place. We can stay there, if we wish, or we can journey out, as Whitman did, to learn about other religions, other ways of defining meaning in the world, and incorporate the most valuable parts of those meanings into the way we see the world and the universe. They become part of us and we become part of them as is so well expressed in "Ulysses," by Alfred Lord Tennyson, a poet whom Whitman greatly admired:

> I am part of all that I have met;
> Yet all experience is an arch where through
> Gleams that untraveled world whose margin fades
> For ever and for ever when I move.
> How dull it is to pause, to make an end,
> To rust unburnished, not to shine in use!
> As though to breathe were life! Life piled on life
> Were all too little, and of one to me
> Little remains; but every hour is saved
> From that eternal silence, something more,
> A bringer of new things; and vile it were
> For some three suns to store and hoard myself,
> And this gray spirit yearning in desire
> To follow knowledge like a sinking star.
> Beyond the utmost bound of human thought.

C

The "Journey motif" is found all through <u>Leaves of Grass</u>, but it finds its most definitive expression in the long poem called "Song of the Open Road." The poet begins the poem:

> Afoot and light-hearted I take to the open road,
> Healthy, free, the world before me,
> The long brown path before me, leading wherever I choose.
>
> Henceforth I ask not good-fortune, I myself am good-fortune,
> Henceforth I whimper no more, postpone no more, need nothing,
> Done with indoor complaints, libraries, querulous criticisms,
> Strong and content I travel the open road.

And then, eight or nine pages later, concludes with these words:

> Allons! The road is before us!
> It is safe—I have tried it—my own feet have tried it well--be not detain'd!
> Let the paper remain on the desk unwritten, and the book on the shelf unopen'd!
> Let the tools remain in the workshop! Let the money remain unearn'd'!
> Let the school stand! Mind not the cry of the teacher!
> Let the preacher preach in his pulpit! Let the lawyer plead in the court, and the judge expound the law.

> Camerado, I give you my hand!
> I give you my love more precious than money,
> I give you myself before preaching or law;
> Will you give me yourself? Will you come travel with me?
> Shall we stick by each other as long as we live?

Between the opening stanzas, where Walt Whitman makes his own personal affirmation, and the closing stanzas, where the poet invites us to join with him "on the road," there are the challenges and the struggles of life, such as pain and death and sorrow and need. "Listen, I will be honest with you," the poet says,

> I do not offer the old smooth prizes, but offer rough new prizes,
> These are the days that must happen to you:
> You shall not heap up what is call'd riches,
> You shall scatter with lavish hand all that you earn or achieve,
> Allons! We must not stop here,
> However sweet the laid-up stores, however convenient this dwelling we cannot remain here,
> However shelter'd this port and however calm these waters we must not anchor here,
> However welcome the hospitality that surrounds us we are permitted to receive it but a little while.

On the journey through life, the poet says, you will "sail pathless and wild seas." To undertake the journey you will need to bring "courage and health" and your journey will be difficult if "you have already spent the best of yourself."

But there are resources "on the road" to help us on our journey. There is the earth that is "sufficient," that is rich with beauty and provides for our needs. There is the air that "serves me with the breath to speak," there is the "light that wraps me and all things in delicate equable showers." But most of all there are the companions along the road, the millions and millions of people on the road who have experienced, as we have experienced, the losses and partings of life, and who can provide comfort. "All seems beautiful to me," the poet sings:

> I can repeat over to men and women, You have done such good to me I would do the same to you,
> I will recruit for myself and you as I go,
> I will scatter myself among men and women as I go,
> I will toss a new gladness and roughness among them,
> Whoever denies me it shall not trouble me,
> Whoever accepts me he or she shall be blessed and shall bless me.

And then there are the "Great Companions." "They too are on the road—they are the swift and majestic men—they are the greatest women." Whitman goes on, in one of his "catalogues," to list employers and sailors and dancers and many others,

> Journeyers gayly with their own youth, journeyers with their bearded and well-grain'd manhood,
> Journeyers with their womanhood, ample, unsurprass'd, content,
> Journeyers with their own sublime old age of manhood or womanhood....

Whitman does not name those we might think of as great – like Jesus or Gautama or Socrates or Confucius – but they are certainly making the journey with us. "They too are on the road." The point of all this is that in our journey through life we have resources available to us from the whole gamut of human existence, from fellow travelers on the road, both living and dead. We all travel the road. "The road is before us." We are all in this together.

D

Walt Whitman's poem, "Song of the Open Road," looks like a new Pilgrim's Progress. It may even be the case that Whitman had John Bunyan's book in mind when he wrote the poem since he possessed a painting by Jesse Talbot which illustrated a scene form Pilgrim's Progress and which the poet thought to be a significant work of art. Whatever may be the case, there is some value to be gained by comparing the two works.

Pilgrim's Progress – the full title is actually Pilgrim's Progress From This World To That Which Is To Come – is an allegory of two pilgrims – Christian and Hopeful—who journey from the City of Destruction to the Celestial City. After a long journey, through many hardships, they finally came within sight of the city. As they neared the city they discovered that they had to cross a deep river, with no bridge over it. "At the sight thereof of this river the pilgrims were much stunned," Bunyan wrote, but some men who had joined them at this time let them know that "You must go through or you cannot come to the gate."

> The pilgrims then, especially Christian, began to despond in his mind, and looked this way and that, but no way could be found by them by which they might escape the river. They then addressed themselves to the river, and entering, Christian began to sink, and, crying out to his good friend

Hopeful, he said, I sink in deep waters; the billows go over my head, all his waves go over me. Selah.

Then said the other, be of good cheer, my brother: I feel the bottom and it is good.

Like Bunyan's pilgrims, Whitman's journeyers on the open road know hardship and despair. But also like "Hopeful" they can discover that at "bottom" the universe is good. "Of the progress of the souls of men and women along the grand roads of the universe, all other progress is the needed emblem and sustenance," the poet writes:

> Forever alive, forever forward,
> Stately, solemn, sad, withdrawn, baffled, mad,
>   turbulent, feeble, dissatisfied,
> Desperate, proud, fond, sick, accepted by men,
>   rejected by men,
> They go! They go! I know that they go, but I know
>   not where they go,
> But I know that they go toward the best—toward
>   something great.

E

There may be echoes of <u>Pilgrim's Progress</u> in Whitman's "road," but there are also some important differences. Hopeful and Christian seek a goal, "the celestial city," defined by a religion formulated in the past. Hopeful and Christian find the confidence they need to make their journey by accepting faith in the Christ revealed two thousand years ago. The "great companions" on Whitman's "road," move not towards the known but toward the unknown. They look for a religious understanding not in the past, but in the future, a future which will be revealed in the journey itself. The pilgrims took a closed route. Whitman's road is "open-ended."

"Now I re-examine philosophies and religions, They may prove well in lecture rooms, yet not prove at all under the spacious clouds and along the landscape and flowing current," Whitman says in "Song of the Open Road."

> Here is the test of wisdom,
> Wisdom is not finally tested in schools,
> Wisdom cannot be pass'd from one having it to another not having it,
> Wisdom is of the soul, is not susceptible of proof, is its own proof,
> Applies to all stages and objects and qualities and is content,
> Is the certainty of the reality and immortality of things, and the excellence of things;
> Something there is in the float of the sight of things that provokes it out of the soul.

Here we arrive at the very heart of the prophetic vision of Walt Whitman.

The religions of the past are not appropriate for the modern world. We must respect them because they served well the people of the past as they made their journeys through life. We must listen to them because they can provide us with insight and help as we make our journey. In a powerful phrase Whitman says that on the "Road" we go about "abstracting the feast yet abstracting not one particle of it." What the poet appears to mean by this is that we must appreciate the "feast" of the past, graciously accept that which nourishes us, but always remember that it is their feast, the feast of the past. It is our journey through time, and through our world, that must provide us with an adequate religious understanding for the living of our days. "From this hour I ordain myself loos'd of limits and imaginary lines," Whitman sings,

> Going where I list, my own master total and absolute,
> Listening to others, considering well what they say,
> Pausing, searching, receiving, contemplating,
> Gently but with undeniable will, divesting myself of the holds that would hold me.

The journey is as "endless as it was beginningless." It is not tied to the past. We must discover the way for ourselves. And Whitman means this in the most personal and individual sense. In the context of Whitman's prophetic vision every person must make decisions for themselves as to the true nature of the universe and its meaning for human existence. "Not I, nor anyone else," he says, "can travel that road for you." "You shall possess the origin of all poems," Whitman sings in "Song of Myself:"

> You shall possess the good of the earth and the sun (there are millions of suns left,)
> You shall no longer take things at second or third hand, nor look through the eyes of the dead, nor feed on specters in books,
> You shall not look through my eyes either, nor take things from me,
> You shall listen to all sides and filter them from your self.

"The sum of all known reverence I add up in you whoever you are," The poet sings in "A Song for Occupations,"

> We consider bibles and religions divine—I do not
>   say they are not divine,
> I say they have grown out of you, and may grow out
>   of you still,
> It is not they who give the life, it is you who give
>   the life.

That is how all of the great religions were born – they were born out of the times and experiences of the people who once lived. A religion for our time, Whitman felt, has to be predicated on our lives and our experiences:

> Will you seek afar off? You surely come back at
>   last,
> In things best know to you finding the best or as
>   good as the best,
>   ....
> Happiness, knowledge, not in another place but this
>   place, not for another hour but this hour.

The journey we must undertake is not a journey fixed in time. It is not a journey defined by the past. It is a perpetual journey into an unknown future. But with companions along the way, like Walt Whitman, we can undertake the journey with hope and with confidence. Perhaps thoughts about that perpetual journey are nowhere more beautifully stated than in "Song of Myself."

> I tramp a perpetual journey (come listen all!)
> My signs are a rain-proof coat, good shoes, and a
>   staff cut from the woods.
> No friend of mine takes his ease in my chair,
> I have no chair, no church, no philosophy,
> I lead no man to a dinner-table, library, exchange,

But each man and each woman of you I lead upon a knoll,
My left hand hooking you round the waist,
My right hand pointing to the landscapes of continents and the public road.

Not I, not any one else can travel that road for you;
You must travel it for yourself.

It is not far, it is within reach.
Perhaps you have been on it since you were born and did not know;
Perhaps it is every where on water and on land.

This day before dawn I ascended a hill and looked at the crowded heaven,
And I said to my spirit, when we become the enfolders of those orbs, and the
pleasure and knowledge of everything in them, shall we be filled and satisfied then?
And my spirit said, No, we but level that lift to pass and continue beyond.

EPILOGUE
THE GERMS OF A GREATER RELIGION

> Poets to come! Orators, singers, musicians to come!
> Not to-day is to justify me and answer what I am for,
> But you, a new brood, native, athletic, continental, greater than before known,
> Arouse! For you must justify me.
> "Poets to Come"

From the time Walt Whitman began work on his great book, <u>Leaves of Grass</u>, he thought in terms of writing a new Bible for a new world. Throughout his life he thought of himself as a poet/prophet who was attempting to articulate a religious vision appropriate for the modern world. He had hoped that the people of America, a land he truly loved, would read his book, accept his vision, and recognize him as a prophet. "The proof of a poet," he wrote in the last words of his preface to the first edition of <u>Leaves of Grass</u>, "is that his country absorbs him as affectionately as he has absorbed it." That did not happen. The nation did not "absorb" his prophetic vision. His book did not become the Bible of the New World.

Perhaps this is always the case. Nobody actually sets out, as Whitman did, to write a Bible. Bibles seem to emerge, over long periods of time, out of the experiences of generations. All one can do, even given a lifetime of struggle and effort and thought, is to make one's contributions and offer them as a gift for the generations who are to follow. In the end, Whitman himself had to realize that he could not complete the task that he had set before himself. All he could do as he says in "Starting from Paumanok" – the series of poems at the beginning of <u>Leaves of Grass</u> which were intended to outline his agenda – was to "drop in the earth the germs of a greater religion."

The completion of the work had to be left to future generations. Walt Whitman planted the "germs of a greater religion" and it was up to others to cultivate them, nurture them, and bring them to full growth so that they could bear fruit.

Walt Whitman knew in the nineteenth century that the world needed prophets who would articulate a religious vision appropriate for the modern world. The need is no less great as we move through the twenty first century. The religious vision of Walt Whitman may not be the place to end as we try to formulate religious values that square with contemporary understandings of the nature of the universe, but it may very well be a good place to begin. The rest is left to the poets and the prophets of the present and the future. They are the ones who must "justify" him. As the great poet says in "Poets to Come":

> I myself but write one or two indicative words for the future,
> I but advance a moment only to wheel and hurry back in the darkness.
> I am a man who, sauntering along without fully stopping, turns a casual look upon you and then averts his face,
> Leaving it to you to prove and define it,
> Expecting the main things from you.

BIBLIOGRAPHY AND ACKNOWLEDGEMENTS

The author gratefully acknowledges his indebtedness to the authors and the publishers of the books listed below. All of the books, or other materials, listed below were consulted in preparation of this manuscript. Every effort has been made to trace the owner(s) and or administrators of copyrighted material, when it was deemed necessary to do so. We regret any omissions and will, upon written notice, make necessary corrections in subsequent printings.

Allen, Gay Wilson, The New Walt Whitman Handbook, New York University Press, New York, 1986.

Allen, Gay Wilson, The Solitary Singer, University of Chicago Press, Chicago, 1985.

Allen, Gay Wilson, A Readers Guide to Walt Whitman, Octagon Books, New York, 1986.

Aspiz, Harold, Walt Whitman and the Body Beautiful, University of Illinois Press, Urbana, 1980.

Barrus, Clara, Whitman and Burroughs, Comrades, Houghton Mifflin Company, Boston, 1931.

Cady, Edwin H. and Budd, Louis J., On Whitman: The Best in American Literature, Duke University Press, Durham, 1987.

Canby, Henry Seidel, Walt Whitman: An American, Houghton Mifflin Co., Boston, 1943.

Carson, Rachel, The Sense of Wonder, Harper and Row, New York, 1965.

Cavitch, David, My Soul and I, Beacon Press, Boston, 1985.

Chaisson, Eric, Untitled quote, used by permission of Eric Chaisson.

Chase, Steward, Walt Whitman Reconsidered, William Sloan Associates, 1955.

Dewey, John, A Common Faith, quoted in Great Companions, Beacon Press, Boston, 1941.

Dubos, Rene, Only One Earth, Norton, New York, 1972.

Ellis, Havelock, The New Spirit, from Leavens, Robert French, Great Companions, Volume II, Beacon Press, Boston, 1941

Eisley, Loren, Darwin's Century, Doubleday, 1958.
    Used by permission of Random House, New York.

Hindus, Milton, Walt Whitman: The Critical Heritage, London: Routledge & Kegan Paul, 1971.

Jastrow, Robert, Until The Sun Dies, W. W. Norton, New York, 1977.

Kuebrich, David, Minor Prophet, Indiana University Press, Bloomington, 1989.

Matthiessen, F.O., American Renaissance, Oxford University Press, New York, 1941.

Miller, Edwin, Walt Whitman's Poetry: A Psychological Journey, New York University Press, New York, 1968.
    Selections quoted used by permission of New York University Press.

Miller, Perry, The Transcendentalists, Harvard University Press, Cambridge, 1977.
    Selections quoted used by permission of the publisher, copyright, 1950, by the President and Fellows of Harvard College.

Montague, Ashley, "The Natural Superiority of Women," The Saturday Review, 1952.
    Used by Permission of AltaMira Press, Lanham, Maryland.

Shapiro, Karl and Miller, James E., in Start With The Sun, University of Nebraska Press, Lincoln,
    Selections quoted used by permission of The University of Nebraska Press.

Stovall, Floyd, The Foreground of Leaves Of Grass, The University Press of Virginia, Charlottesville, 1974.

Untermeyer, Louis, The Poetry and Prose of Walt Whitman, Simon and Schuster, New York, 1949.

Weston, Robert Terry, "Our of The Stars."
    Used by permission of Dick Weston Jones.

Zweig, Paul Walt Whitman, The Making of a Poet, Viking, New York, 1984.

Printed in the United States
152528LV00002B/34/A